True Brothers

True Brothers
A Guide to the Practice of Ásatrú in Prison

First Edition: Summer 2002

Edred
General Editor

Copyright © 2014
by Lodestar

All rights reserved. No part of this book, either in part or in whole, may be reproduced, transmitted or utilized in any form or by any means electronic, photographic or mechanical, including photocopying, recording, or by any information storage and retrieval system, without the permission in writing from the Publisher, except for brief quotations embodied in literary articles and reviews.

For permissions, or for the serialization, condensation, or for adaptation write the Publisher at the address below.

Lodestar
P. O. Box 16
Bastrop, Texas 78602
USA

www.seekthemystery.com

Abbreviations

BCE Before the Common Era (= B.C.)
CE   Common Era (= A.D.)
OE   Old English (also called Anglo-Saxon)
ON   Old Norse

A Note to Readers

This is the first edition of *True Brothers*. If you have any ideas or information about how subsequent editions of this book could be improved, based on your own experience, send a letter care of the publisher.

Table of Contents

Introduction	vi
Chapter One: History of the Faith and Folk	1
Chapter Two: The Worlds	8
Chapter Three: The Divinities	11
Chapter Four: The Soul	16
Chapter Five: The Holy Stead	21
Chapter Six: The Rites	23
Chapter Seven: Kindreds	42
Chapter Eight: Your Rights	47
Glossary	49
Bibliography	52

Introduction

Over the years of conducting business at Rûna-Raven Press we have come to see the level of need among incarcerated or imprisoned folk for a good guide to the practice of the faith of Odinism, Ásatrú, or the troth. This need can best be filled by the pen of Edred— who is generally acknowledged as the leading authority on the old religion of our ancestors.

The purpose of this book is to provide a general guide to the practice of the old Germanic faith in the prison setting. This guide is not only the outer practice of the religion, but also to certain inner aspects often neglected. This book contains many pointers never before revealed— pointers that will also be of great interest to all followers of the old ways. *True Brothers* cannot be a comprehensive, or total guide to all aspects of the religion, of course. But it can act as the main guide to incarcerated souls— both for outer action as well as inner direction. This little book contains the basic major tenets of the religion, an outline of its important articles of faith, and a complete discussion of the major rituals of the troth, or Ásatrú.

Prison officials and chaplains should be encouraged to read this book as well. It helps make the case for the legitimacy of the faith apart from the misunderstandings that often rage around Ásatrú— for example that it is a "cover" for "gang" activity, or that it is basically a "racist" ideology. Neither of these things are true as we outline the religion in these pages.

It is our belief that the mainstays of the religion can be stated simply and profoundly in a few pages and that these pages can be the basis for deeper and further study and inner experience. It is true that the religion of Odinism is a religion of *doing*, of action. But a form of action is also *thought*. In fact all true and good action must begin with a thought. Let the words in this little book be your thought-guide to action. Whether you are in prison for a short time, or a life-time, the period you spend isolated from the rest of the world can act as a crucible of personal transformation. This transformation is only possible, however, once you consciously determine that you will follow the way of Odin and study and dedicate your life to the pursuit of the Secret (the Rune) which is the key to your own rebirth. You can use the time you have in prison to hone criminal skills— which will only hasten your ultimate demise— or you can determine here and now to follow the Right Way and become a fighter in the cause of the All-Father. Most essential to that fight is your own personal discipline and transformation. All men, whether incarcerated or not, have the same basic choice in life: to follow the Right, and possibly become a winner in life and enter Walhalla, or to succumb to the Wrong and have their souls dwindle away in Hel.

If you have chosen to do the Right— read on.

The Directory of Rûna-Raven Press

Chapter One

History of the Faith and Folk

The faith of troth, or Ásatrú, or Odinism, or whatever name one wishes to all the ancient and ancestral faith of our ancestors, is one that reaches back into the dawn of time, and one that has always been the deep underlying religion of our people— regardless of whether they have come to think of themselves as "Christians." As such its essence lies outside the realm of "history" as we usually think of this term. The old way, the old faith, is with us always because it is an intrinsic part of who we are— body and soul.

But there are certain historical traces of the old way, which are important for us to study and understand if we are to make our intrinsic and innate faith strong and informed. It is like the old way is a seed in each of us, but knowledge is the water and sunlight which cause it to grow up in us and reach beyond the surface of our unconscious minds. When the seedling is well-fed, it will break up into the light of our mental awareness— and we will realize it was in us all the time. But without the water and light of good information, the seed will not rightly grow.

Ancient History

The periods of the ancient history of our people is divided into various "ages." These are the Archaic Age (±700 BCE to the beginning of our era), the Older Roman Age (to about 200 CE), the Younger Roman Age (200-400 CE), the Migration Age (400-800), and the Viking Age (800-1100). Little is known of the religion practiced by in the Archaic Age. We do know, however, that the Germanic peoples are a branch of the large Indo-European family of languages and peoples. By studying the greater and more archaic Indo-European mythic and cultural traditions we learn more about the origin and background of the earliest Germanic peoples. The other Indo-European peoples include the Indians and Iranians in the east and the Celts, Italics, Slavs and Greeks in the west. Our knowledge of the Indo-Europeans, our oldest ancestors, goes back to a time before the pyramids in Egypt were built. We will periodically refer to Indo-European patterns of thought in our discussions of various topics in this book.

Roman Ages

The Roman Age are marked from the time when the Roman historians and ethnographers first took notice of the northern peoples they called the Germani. As early as 113 BCE the Empire of Rome was invaded by northern tribes called the Cimbri and Teutones, who came from the northern part of what is now known as Denmark. It is especially from that time forward we learn of the Germanic peoples first from descriptions of them given in Greek and Latin sources. The reference to the religion of the Germanic peoples found in these accounts have been conveniently collected and translated by James Chisholm in his *Grove and Gallows* (Rûna-Raven, 2002).

The Romans were never able to conquer the Germanic peoples. In his book about his own exploits in Gaul (then the Celtic country that now more or less corresponds to France) Julius Caesar reports about the customs of the Germans. His book, *On the Gallic War* (*De bello gallico*) was written about 50 BCE. Caesar says that the Germans have "no druids," by which he meant they had no exclusive priest-class, as the Romans and Celts had. The king or the head of each family and clan functioned as a priest on the holy occasions. He also comments about how the Germans will band together in times of war and give their undivided allegiance to a war-leader until the end of the war. The Celts, on the other hand, were easy to divide and conquer, because they would not offer their allegiance in such a way.

At one point the Romans were even decisively defeated by the Germans under their war-leader Arminius in the famous battle of the Teutoburger Forest in the year 9 CE. Arminius is the origin of the famous "Hermann the German." Germania north of the Danube and east of the Rhine was never Romanized and Scandinavia remained entirely free of Roman political and military influence— although trade and other forms of peaceful interaction between all parts of Germania and Greece and Rome (as well as the eastern realms of the Iranians) was lively.

Germanic religion in the Roman Age is perhaps best described by the Roman historian in his famous book on the Germanic peoples: *Germania* (written about 97 CE). All of his observations are not accurate, as he was writing for his own Roman readership, and was not a skilled firsthand observer of Germanic religious practices. The text of the *Germania* must be read and studied with critical attention to each line.

Migration Age

By around 400 CE the Germanic tribes had already begun to move southward throughout Europe, The Goths had come down into what is now Russia from Scandinavia much earlier, around 150 CE, and had set up kingdoms in what is now Russia. The Goths, along with the Vandals, form what are called the Eastern Germanic peoples. The Scandinavians form the Northern Germanic branch, while the Germans (and hence Anglo-Saxons) form the Southern or Western branch. The period in which the various Germanic tribes moved from north of the Danube and east of the Rhine to create kingdoms in what had been the Roman Empire is called the "Migration Age."

During this time many tribes were created, and many migrated to new homes. The Angles, Saxons and Jutes left the mainland of Germany and colonized what is now England (= Angla-land). The Franks moved into Gaul and created what is now France (Franc-ia). The Ostrogoths created a new kingdom in Italy— the first post-Imperial political state on the Italian peninsula. In southern Gaul and northern Spain the Visigoths, who sacked the Roman capital in 410 CE, established a kingdom that would last until the Muslim invasion in 711. The Swabians had a kingdom in western Spain, and the Vandals had one that stretched from southern Spain (Andalusia = Vandalusia) to northern Africa.

While the North Germanic peoples would remain entirely heathen for centuries to come, the tribes that became parts of the what had been the Roman Empire officially converted to Christianity. But most of them "converted" to their *own kind* of Christianity, originated among the Goths. This "Gothic Church" largely retained the old beliefs but dressed them up in Christian appearances. They followed the Arian doctrine (so-called after bishop Arius) which emphasized Jesus as merely a man who had perfected himself, denied the doctrine of the Trinity, and de-emphasized the idea of "original sin." Eventually the Germanic peoples who remained in the south were converted to Roman Christianity. The first Germanic tribe to become Roman Catholic was the Franks. Because of this they became the arsenal of the church and began a new Roman Empire — the so-called Holy Roman Empire — in the year 800 CE.

At the conclusion of the Migration Age its history is marked by the Frankish conquests of the Germanic tribes east of the Rhine: the Frisians, Alemanni, Bavarians, Thuringians and the continental Saxons. In these conquests in the name of the church, the vanquished were offered a choice between Christian baptism and death. On one day near a place called Verden there were many Saxons who preferred beheading to baptism.

During this period the far north of Scandinavia was flourishing and was largely free from any Christian influence.

Viking Age

In the time just before 800 CE Northern Germanic peoples began to raid and trade far and wide by sea. Around 793 a group of Norwegian raiders, called *vikingar* in their own language, looted the monastery at Lindisfarne on the eastern coast of England. This is the event and official date of he inception of the so-called "Viking Age." We put "Viking Age" in quotes because it can be misleading. A viking is a raider and/or trader. The term does not describe a whole culture, but rather just one part of a larger culture, viewed primarily from the outsider's perspective. The typical viking was a farmer or minor king in his homeland in Norway, Denmark or Sweden. At certain times of the year — usually the spring and summer — he would organize raiding and trading missions. These were made possible by their vastly superior shipbuilding craftsmanship. Their ships could easily travel over vast open stretches of ocean they came as far as North America around 1000 CE), and at the same time were shallow enough to go up rivers with ease and were even light enough to be carried overland by their crews to go from river to river in the vast expanse of what became Russia.

We are best informed about the religious beliefs and myths of the North Germanic, or Norse, peoples during this historical period because of the survival of a large body of their poetry recorded in the *Poetic Edda* and in skaldic poetry of the time.

"Conversion"

The whole process of "conversion" has been largely misunderstood by many historians. More recently historians, such as James Russell, have developed a more accurate and sophisticated view of this historical process. Earlier it was often thought that a people was converted to Christianity, and pretty much from that time forward they were somehow convinced of the validity of the new religion. This is wrong on a number of counts. First, whole peoples do not "convert" to a religion. Only individuals can do this. Second, even individuals cannot really understand a set of concepts that are largely alien to the mind-set the individual brings to the situation. This is why even individuals who wanted to be Christians in the Middle Ages were far more pagan in their outlooks than most modern pagans are today. Third, whole populations take centuries to really convert to a new religion. James Russell estimated that Europe did not become truly Christian until around 1500 CE. For the most part the old pagan or heathen beliefs and practices simply continued on in Christian guise for several centuries, often right up to today.

Christianization of the various Germanic tribes occurred under a variety of circumstances. The Goths were Christianized, as has been mentioned, under their own form of Christianity. This eventually died out under unrelenting attack from the Roman Catholics. Some tribes, such as the Franks and Anglo-Saxons were Christianized when their king officially converted to Christianity (and was baptized). This is because generally in ancient times the king was the highest priest of the religion as well, and the folk followed his religious lead. Other areas, such as the Continental Saxons and other central European Germans, were Christianized by force of conquest. Iceland had the unusual distinction of being a place where the legislature, or Thing, actually voted to become Christian officially. (This was done under enormous economic and cultural pressure, and was not at first binding on private practice.)

Survivals

Because the Christianization process was so haphazard and political, traditional pre-Christian cultural patterns largely continued under the cover of official Christian symbols for many generations. The old heroes, gods and goddesses were often worshipped under the guise of Christian "saints." For example, the patron saint of both Germany and England is St. George. Now the Germanic hero is and always was a dragon slayer— Siegfried, or Beowulf, for example. Therefore for the Christian patron to be taken seriously by the folk he had to be a dragon slayer too. St. George had no story about killing a dragon attached to his legend until he became the patron saint of the Germans and English— then all of a sudden a story about his dragon-slaying exploits were included by the church.

There is in fact a whole system of correspondences between the Christian saints and the old Germanic gods and goddesses. This pattern is seen everywhere in Christendom where the religion displaces a traditional faith.

Customs survived as well. In one way or another the practice of putting up a "Christmas tree' is a survival of the ancient Germanic Yule-tide custom of decorating trees (usually in the forests and sacred groves) to attract ancestral spirits (alfs) to receive gifts. The church eventually outlawed such practices, but for a time the folk simply brought the tree indoors where it could be hidden. The focus shifted from the ancestors to the children— who in the ancient Germanic idea of rebirth — were the ancestors *reborn*.

History of the "Revivals"

It is most often not accurate to speak of the "revival" of Germanic spiritual values, because in fact they never fully died out. It is more like they have gone to sleep to one degree of another— awaiting the right conditions to occur in individuals and groups of individuals of the values to be *reawakened*. This process of reawakening began almost as soon as the old ways were ousted from their established places in our culture. In medieval times men like Snorri Sturluson kept the old myths and legends alive. While in the early modern period men such as Johannes Bureus actually began to try to reawaken the spiritual and magical values and practices of the ancients. Bureus, for example worked around 1600, when the Edda was hardly known.

The true movements of reawakening began in earnest during the so-called Romantic phase of European culture. This cultural model might better have been called "Germanticism," because it was generally adhered to by the Germans and English. Romanticism is characterized by a general turning inward to the soul of the individual and to the soul of the nation. Romantics have been called nature-worshippers, and this label might fit if we understand it completely. The Latin word *natio*, which gives us both the words "nation" and "nature," has to do with what is born, *native*, *innate*. They clearly saw that ideas were somehow mysteriously encoded in the "blood" of the individual and in the collective blood of the nation. This concept linked in an objective way the soul of the individual and the collective culture of the nation. This essential and profound reality had been obscured by centuries of Christian doctrine. In order for Christianity to at all seem credible, it had to disassociate the soul of the individual from the collective body of the folk. This is also the origin of our modernistic hyper-individualistic anti-culture. In reality most *modern* values are merely secularized Christian patterns of thought.

In the latter part of the 1700s, and at the beginning of the 1800s the Romantic school evidenced great interest in native traditions of all sorts, which included the native traditions of the pre-Christian ancestors of the Romantics themselves. The Romantic turned his interests inward to matters of the mind to and soul as well as to the natural and organic roots of life. In Germany two important leaders of the Romantic movement were Jacob and Wilhelm Grimm. They were pioneers in the academic world of linguistics and comparative religion and mythology, as well as being the founders of the discipline of folklore. They collected their folk tales and established the idea that the old ways had been somehow suppressed below the surface of contemporary society. It was their nationalistic purpose to liberate these patterns from this state so that they could help reform the contemporary culture of Germany.

The most serious efforts at actually reawakening the old Germanic spirit at this time was underway in Scandinavia— especially in Denmark and Sweden. Many of the greatest poets and thinkers in Scandinavia were devotees of the Northern aesthetic. It was especially in Sweden where actual organizations were formed to reawaken the spiritual heritage of the north. Most prominent of these were the *Manhems Förbund* and the *Götisk Förbund*. These groups had rituals and doctrines of a complex nature.

In the latter part of the 1800s the German composer and artist Richard Wagner created a mytho-poetic vision based on the tales of the ancient Germanic gods and goddesses and on the knightly virtues of the High Middle Ages.

Toward the beginning of the 20th century the idea of Germanic religion and its revival was becoming extremely popular in Germany. This was not an underground or "counter-cultural" movement of the kind we might have found in the Anglo-Saxon world at the time. The German and Austrian "revivalists" were a part of the establishment oriented-culture of the day. Chief among these revivalists was Guido von List. List created a society for the restoration of the old Germanic culture and wrote a number of books on the subject from a mystical and esoteric angle. There were many other efforts at creating a truly Germanic religion at this time.

In the midst of the great enthusiasm for all things Germanic in the early part of the 20th century, and in the wake of the "War to End All Wars" (WWI) there arose a political movement popularly called Nazism— or more properly National Socialism. Individuals within this movement were perhaps sympathetic to, or had indeed to some degree been shaped by, some of the heroic Germanic ideology of the 19th century. However, the National Socialist movement in general was not sympathetic to Germanic heathenism. Hitler mocked the "Wotan worshippers," and made pacts with the Catholic Church. The Nazis for the most part simply *used* the symbols of Germanic antiquities such as the runes or the "swastika," but were really enamored of the Roman Empire— the ancient rival of the Germanic folk. However, anti-German and anti-Germanic propagandists — both *during* the war and *after* — have constantly tried to connect the idea of Germanic paganism to the National Socialism. Today's Ásatrú/Odinism has nothing to do with the ideology of National Socialism or "Nazism."

Post-War Movement

In the years following the Second World War the whole idea of Germanic culture has been saddled with the effects of the unrelenting propaganda campaign originated in the years of that war. This is the main reason why although there were millions of people involved with the pre-war movement, by comparison the movement to reawaken Germanic culture in the latter part of the 20th century has been very small indeed. We can now work to see that the movement regains the momentum lost in the wake of the Second World War.

If what the propagandists said was true: that the militaristic and governmental excesses of the Third Reich were traceable to "Germanic heathenism" that would be one thing, but such is simply not the case. The "Third Reich" is a Roman concept, and almost all of Nazi ideology is traceable to the Roman concepts of centralized Imperial power. The Edda bears no traces of the hallmarks of National Socialist ideology: imperial political aims and anti-Semitism.

In the 1970s there began a new movement for the restoration of Germanic religion. These were led by such men as Sveinbjörn Beinteinsson in Iceland, John Yeowell in England, and Stephen McNallen in North America. Ásatrú started very small indeed. By the late 1980s it had expanded beyond the scope of the few small groups that had pioneered it in the 1970s— sometimes not for the better. There are now dozens of groups charged with the responsibility of re-establishing the ancestral ways. None is dominant over the others. The whole troth, or the religion, continues to grow slowly and at a grass-roots level.

As a true brother, you can help this movement and participate in the world-historical events in a number of ways, depending on what your circumstances are.

Prisoners can be divided into three groups: those who are gong to be released in a fairly short time (under five years), those who are in prison for the foreseeable future (5-20 years), and those who will not likely be released. Depending on where you find yourself in these possibilities, you can participant in the greater movement in a variety of ways. All men, regardless of their circumstances, are charged wit the responsibility to make themselves *better*. The inner work of forging a relationship with the gods and goddesses and with your ancestors, of following the path of the Nine Noble Virtues, is eternally valid for all men at all times. The question, however, arises as to how you can participate in the effort to re-establish our ancestral ways in Midgard.

If you are going to be released in a short time: prepare yourself diligently for the time of your release. Educate yourself, dedicate yourself to the idea that when you are once more walking free in Midgard you will not forget the commitments you made to yourself and to your gods while in prison. Learn what you can of a practical nature in prison, learn what you can of the lore. Plan to participate in the religious organization of your choice in Midgard.

If you are going to be in prison for a number of years more, you must use this time wisely. Think of the prison as a sort of monastery of the troth— a place where you can forge your mind and your self into a transformed entity. You will have to do a good deal more work while in prison, because when you get out your time will be shorter in Midgard.

Those who have come to the conclusion that they will be spending most of the rest of their lives in prison have a special, virtually *magical* function in the movement: it is their work to focus the force of the gods on the expansion of the voice of the gods in Midgard, and to educate those whom you meet in prison who will one day find their ways back to Midgard.

You now find yourself in a physically demanding circumstance. However, let it be understood that the fight we have to win at this time in the world is not a physical fight. The days of using physical force to fight our battles has receded into the past. Today we must fight by means of ideas, the media, education, and so on. Being "suckered" into a physical confrontation with physically overpowering forces is a trap. A trap we cannot afford to have our men pulled into— no matter how "tempting" it might seem on the spur of the moment.

Thus we see the history of our troth in terms of your place in it. What has gone before is but a prelude to what you will forge now. Work with us, work with your brothers in Midgard to re-establish our ancestral ways.

Chapter Two

The Worlds

It is of essential importance for the true brother to be aware of the inner nature of the world or cosmos: how it came into being, how it is ordered, and how worlds end. The reason for this is that for a man to become a man of knowledge, he must come to know who he is and where he finds himself in his total environment. Then he can come to learn how to develop and develop in the world and in himself. This chapter is devoted to the problem of the nature of the world, or the environment in which your soul is situated.

Cosmogony: How the World Came to Be

In the beginning there was nothing but a magically charged void, called *ginnunga-gap* in Old Norse. This space contains the whole cosmos in a potential, but undifferentiated and "chaotic" form. Here energy and mass are evenly mixed and no one thing is differentiated from another. In this state there occurs a polarization of forces— poetically referred to as "fire" and "ice" in the mythology. The two opposing forces at the two extreme "ends" of space converge in the middle of space and create a mild coming together of extremes. In that place, the ice is vivified by the sparks of life and the world of nature comes into being. But it is still unordered by consciousness.

Various entities inhabit this space. They are called "giants" (or more technically, thurses and etins). The original and greatest of these entities is the immense Ymir, whose body makes up a large part of space. Through generations of evolution these entities eventually give birth to the first truly conscious beings: the first Æsir— the triad of Odin-Vili-Ve. The conscious mind of Odin sees the chaotic and unconscious way things are and sees that they could be better. He sacrifices Ymir and re-creates the world according to a rational, conscious pattern of law and order. However, the world is created as a result of a crime— the killing of a kinsman. This is why, according to our tradition, the cosmos is doomed to ultimate destruction, because no crime goes uncompensated for. (See the section on *ørlög*.)

Cosmology: How the World Is

Odin, working in his triadic form, slays Ymir and uses the various parts of his body to fit out his newly designed cosmos— this is a way of mythically saying that the mass and energy were redistributed in a rational pattern by the god of consciousness. When the process was complete the world could be seen to be arranged in a "tree-like" pattern. No ancient diagram like the one below has survived, however, it is clear from verbal descriptions that this pattern was well-known to the Germanic peoples. Asgard and the realm of the elves is always described as being "above," while Hel and the realm of the dwarves is always described as being "below," or under the ground. Niflheim or the mist-world of ice is described in the north, and the realm of fire, Muspell, is always seen in the south. The realm of the etins is consistently said to be in the east— for example when a thunderstorm is racing from the west toward the east the people say: "Redbeard (= Thorr) is faring east to slay the etins." By the same token the realm of the Vanir is consistently seen to be in the west. When all of these factors are put together the image produced below emerges as the traditional pattern of the cosmos as envisioned by our ancestors.

This model can be seen as a something that on one level is easily understood by any child, and at the same time it contains powerful secrets of astrophysics. That is the nature of a Traditional system. It is not bound by time or space. It is eternally valid and is not subject to "scientific verification" nor can it ever be "disproven." It is mythic, it is poetic, it is something of the soul as well as of the world. He who makes it a part of himself will be blessed with great gifts.

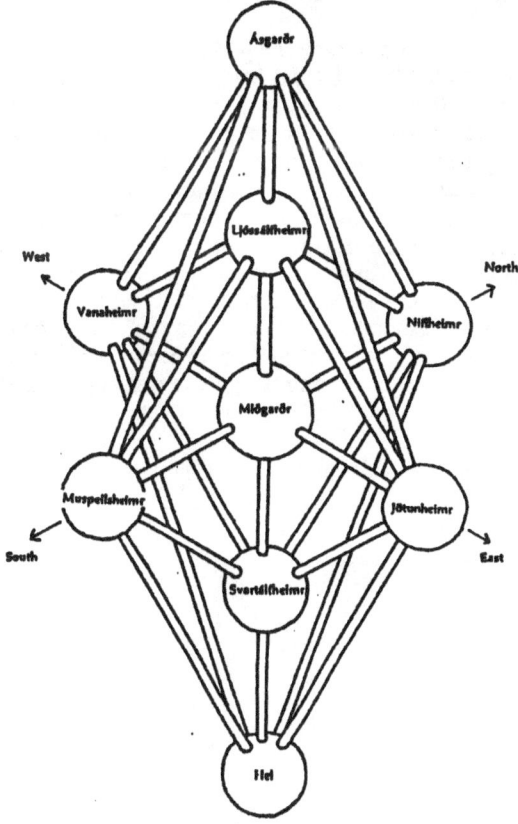

The Yggdrasill Model of the Cosmos

Eschatology: How Worlds End

As was said before, because the cosmos was shaped as a result of a "crime" and because all crimes, regardless of whether they are "legally prosecuted" or not, will be "punished" — that is there will eventually be *justice*, or a re-balancing of the scale in the cosmos — the crime which set the world into motion is the cause of its ultimate collapse. Ymir's slaying is the origin of the cosmos, but it is also the cause for the end of the world, or the *ragnarök*. There is nothing to lament in this, thus it must be, thus shall it always be.

Worlds come and go in existence all the time. The *ragnarök* is not necessarily something we are looking for in world history, such as the Christians are fond of doing. We understand that every time a man dies, there is a *ragnarök*, every time a nation crumbles, there is a *ragnarök*. A *ragnarök* is simply thought of as the last phase of any cyclical development— it is rarely pleasant. However, those who have true understanding can often ride it out, and even survive the effects of such a "catastrophe."

In the mythology we learn of how the gods are confronted by their opposites: Odin by the Fenris Wolf, Thorr by the Midgard Serpent, and so on. All of the polarized opposites in the cosmic order turn in on themselves and the fragile forces of consciousness represented by the gods and goddesses are "destroyed." That is the development that the forces of consciousness have established are destroyed, but the seeds of who and what they are cannot be destroyed. The seed of the divine is small and fragile, the mass of the giants is vast and powerful. But it is the smallness and the fragility of the divine spark in the cosmos which gives it its eternal strength. The realm of the giants is vast and continuous, but the realm of divine consciousness is limited and subject to complex laws of development and re-development. In order for the divine spark to survive it must follow its function: it must *think* and be aware of itself. It is by thinking and through self-awareness that the cosmic struggle is eternally waged.

Chapter Three

The Divinities

It is a chief difference between traditional religions and the "revealed" religions such as Judaism, Christianity and Islam, that in traditional religions as long as the adherent holds that the gods, goddesses and myths embody and encode the deepest truths and that the adherent claims loyalty (troth) with these gods and myths, that that adherent can not be called a "heretic" or "unbeliever." In the troth there is truly no "heresy" as long as a man claims to be true to the old gods (as he understands them), then that man is to be called *true*. We see this same pattern in other traditional folk-religions alive and well in the world today— such as Hinduism and Shinto.

The divinities are arranged according to their *functions*, that is according to their characteristic actions or essences. This arrangement is one that is inherited from the oldest level of Indo-European ideology. It is most pronounced in the Germanic and Indo-Aryan branches of the Indo-European heritage. Just as a man must have a head, a thinking apparatus to govern his body and govern the events of his life, so too must the gods be ruled by the essence of sovereign — kingly — power. Sovereign power is characterized by thought and self-awareness. In the mythology we see that the so-called "first function," that of the sovereign, is sub-divided into two categories: that of the Judge-King, who thinks and rules with a rational mind, and the Priest-Magician, who is self-aware and governs with inspiration. In the Germanic mythology these are Tyr and Odin respectively. However, in the course of time, already in the ancient period, Odin had begun to subsume the function of Tyr— as well as other functions in the pantheon. This is because Odin is a god of synthesis of opposites. He can therefore fairly easily assimilate characteristics which are not originally his own. For this reason too, he is an ideal god of self-transformation.

The second function is that of physical power or strength. In the mythology this function is filled by the god Thorr. Thorr is the Warrior of the gods. Historically he was not so much a god *of* warriors, but he is the warrior of the gods themselves. It is his function to protect the realm of the gods and to keep the perimeters of the space in which conscious, divine power can manifest itself safe and secure. The second function is always under the strict control of the first function.

The third function of the gods is that of Production and Reproduction. Without this function the gods, as well as humans, would cease to even exist— and so the whole divine order, which forms a matrix in which consciousness can exist and evolve, would collapse. For this reason the third function is of extreme importance.

The first and second functions are filled by the Æsir, while the third function if that of the Vanir. The whole ideology of the functions of the gods and goddesses in the Germanic system of the divine order forms a powerful and eternal metaphysic which can guide the world is wise ways, be it in the area of psychology and personal development, or in the area of law and social and cultural order. The doctrine of the functions of the gods is the guidepost to a healthy and happy order in the world.

The whole subject of the gods and goddesses is most difficult, actually impossible, to address in strictly logical terms. This is because personal manifestations invite deep personal relationships between the divinities and individual true brothers. Each of these relationships is unique, and no general, universally correct statements can be made on the gods and goddesses at this living level. What can be said is that the gods and goddesses are REAL, there are many of them, they are ordered in a sort of divine society, and that they are as dependent on us for their continuing existence as we are for our being.

What are the gods and goddesses? To this question there can be many answers. Much depends on the level of understanding any one true man or woman has at any one time. REAL gods, like REAL people, are not one-dimensional easily defined pigeonholed entities. Some understand the gods as pure mental or psychological constructs, some as true living beings, and others as forces of nature. Ásatrú does not place limits or impose types of understanding true folk must hold on this. To be true one must only trust in the gods and goddesses and see to it that they are honored in an evenhanded way— each according to its dignity in the ordering of the divinities. Individuals will have their favorite gods and goddesses who are often worshipped together.

The idea of having many gods and goddesses may seem "primitive" to some. But really it is "ultra-modern"— or "post"-modern (and actually timeless). Today, in our post-Christian world, we are already and quite naturally falling back on our old system of many gods. In a so-called pluralistic society we allow for many life-styles, value systems, and so forth. For each of these there is very often and quite naturally an icon or symbol of some kind which serves as a focus for that value system. In real terms that is a sign of the god or goddess behind that value system. The various gods and goddesses are to some extent living centers of deep seated values— within individuals and within the whole culture. Only one example of this will suffice to show what is meant here. It is not by accident that we call our iconic female sex symbols "goddesses"— for through them is manifested the power of the Lady Freyja. Her living form is used to sell everything from automobiles (another divine icon = the horse) to toothpaste. If you need proof of the true existence of the gods and goddesses, look around with open eyes and they will overwhelm you with their presence.

In the elder wisdom, it was known that that which made men and women human was a set of divine gifts given by the gods at the birth of humanity ("Völuspá" 17-18). Through and within these gifts we know the gods directly— for it is that we share with them. The gods and goddesses are therefore seen as the divine ancestors. We are, in one way or another, descended from them— body and soul. This is also the real reason why, no matter what we do, we can not really "break with the gods." Ours is not a "contractual" relation-ship— it is one of *blood*. So long as we exist, the gods and goddesses exist.

There are two main classes or families of the gods. The Æsir and the Vanir. Their power intermingles on many levels, since although they are distinct from one another on one level, on another level the Æsir have taken in the Vanir, and they form one vast realm of the gods with two poles of power. In the Æsir are centered the powers of consciousness and forces under the control of consciousness, while in the Vanir are centered the organic powers of nature. The intermingling of these two poles defines the nature of the human experience, how they effectively and rightly intermingle and relate to the human experience is the essence of the troth.

The Æsir
Odin

Of all the gods of the Germanic peoples it must be said that Odin is the highest and most mighty. His might and main is that of the soul and mind. He is the giver of the spiritual gifts that allow us to know and understand ourselves and the world— and this is the root of his supremacy. It is mainly for this reason that he is called the All-Father. He is the god of the runes (mysteries), ecstasy, poetry, magic, death, and a hundred other things besides. His names number in the hundreds also, for all that we can name has something of Odin in it. To approach Odin it takes a brave — and perhaps foolhardy — soul. This is because he is as fickle and as mysterious as the workings of our own minds. Odin is the ultimate god of the sovereign power of kings and priests— that which is the power to bring all things, no matter how diverse they seem, together in a meaningful way. But in ancient times, although his primacy was acknowledged, he was not a *popular* god. Only those who were *chosen* followed him— often to apparent disaster.

Tyr

Also high and mighty is the god Tyr. He is the god of the rational mind, and rules over our abilities to reason and to come to good judgments. It is his power that is behind the ordering of the rational laws of the cosmos and of human society. Tyr is the god of true law and order. This is also a quality much valued among the sovereign powers. Tyr can only judge that which is right and give his favor to that, but our innate trust in our rightness leads us to call on him for victory. In doing so we make as much a statement of trust in our own selves as we do in Tyr himself. Tyr is also the spirit of giving of the individual self to serve the interest of the whole. This also set Tyr apart from the masses. His path is a demanding, and sometimes thankless, one.

Thorr

Thorr is the ancient war-god, although he is not necessarily the main god among all warriors themselves. But he eternally holds this position among the gods themselves. It is he who is their chief defender— with his mighty hammer Mjolnir he defends the law and order of Asgard and Midgard. He is steadfast and true and can be relied on above all other gods. His chief power is that of *physical* strength. He embodies all the raw physical power in the world— in the service of the gods and humanity.

Frigga

Among the goddesses the greatest is said to be Frigga. She is the queen of the goddesses and seems to hold them all together in an orderly fashion. She is no simple goddess of fertility, as some might try to make her. Her power holds the social fabric together and she sees to domestic order— within the realms of the gods as well as in Midgard.

The Vanir
Njordr

The father of Freyja and Freyr, or the Lady and the Lord, is a mysterious figure named Njordr. He is mysterious because Tacitus reports that the Germanic peoples had a goddess named Nerthus, but in the Viking Age we find the name reflected as a masculine god. It is likely that this entity is an androgynous being capable of re-producing itself— and thus is the ultimate Van in the sense that it is able to control the entire process of reproduction within itself. Njordr is the god of the wealth and riches derived from the sea.

Freyja

Among the Vanir (Vanir) the goddess Freyja is the foremost. Her name means simply "the Lady." She is said to be equal in power with Frigga, but they are very different in character. In her are embodied the powers of magic, sexual love, cyclical development, and war. She knows the form of magic called seidh— which she is said to have taught to Odin. Freyja is the mistress of eroticism, which goes beyond "fertility," and into the realm of the power of sexuality itself. Her power in the area of fertility comes from the fact that she rules over the process of thing coming into being, growing and passing away to a new arising. This is the turn of the year that leads to wealth and well being. In this she works in tandem with her twin brother, Freyr. As half of the warriors slain in battle go to Valhalla to be in Odin's army, the other half go to Freyja, to be with her in Folkvang. Among the Vanir, Freyja brings all things together in a sort of hidden realm, much as Odin does among the Æsir.

Freyr

Freyja has a twin brother, Freyr, whose name means "the Lord." As Freyja is involved with hidden workings among the Vanir, Freyr, along with his father/mother Njordr, rules over the outer forms. He embodies the manifest powers of wealth, well-being, peace, and pleasure. He is the chief ruler of these things in the world itself. Therefore he is called the God, or Lord, of This-World, so it is easy to see why he, along with his sister Freyja were probably the most popular divinities in the north for the bulk of the people. Among the Vanir, Freyr is a reflection of the kingly power embodied in Tyr and Odin among the Æsir.

It is most typical for individual true brothers to explore the tales and myths of the gods and goddesses, to meditate on them, and to begin to develop deep inner connections with one or several of the divinities. In nights of yore, of course, this was probably something done in childhood, as the tales of the gods and goddesses would have been well known to all. In our present world, however, this learning must be an act of will.

From these brief descriptions it can be seen that the gods and goddesses of the troth form a profound "community of power" that is quite intricately interwoven. There are threads running through and among the gods and goddesses that show how they are related to one another and how they work together.

The gods and goddesses of our ancestors, whatever they were, still dwell within us. They live as long as we live. They can be put to sleep, they can be silenced, but they cannot be killed, unless the thread of organic being stretching from generation to generation that they set into motion — the life of the folk itself — be ended. The work of Ásatrú is the reawakening of the slumbering of the gods and goddesses. That they have been stirred already, has already been shown by some unfortunate events of this century. As unpleasant an ineffective as these events proved to be, they are still signs of a fully living divine power. No other "revivalist" movement can claim anything close to these signs of vitality.

Those who are true must now nurture the already manifest vitality. This is done through the working of blessings, the giving of gifts on a regular basis, and most importantly the development of our own minds and hearts to be able to hear and understand rightly the words and ways of the gods and goddesses as they begin to become real within us. The horn of the self must be made strong so that when the power of the gods flows into it it will not burst asunder. With each blessing rightly done, with each gift rightly given, we grow even stronger.

Chapter Four

The Soul

Our ancestors had extremely complex traditions about the nature and structure of the human being. This structure included parts of the human being which are visible and those that are generally invisible. The distinction between body and soul was not as cut and dried as it seems to most people today. The physical and spiritual "parts" of the human being were arrayed in a kind of spectrum, and we should really not talk of a physiology separate from a psychology, but rather make a study of what we call the psychosomatic (or soul-body) complex.

This complex doctrine of the soul can be compared with that of the Christians, which is generally an extremely impoverished view of the human soul. Christian doctrine only recognizes the "spirit," "soul" and "body," with the soul and spirit forming something entirely separate from the body. Where the Christian doctrine has only three terms, the traditional Germanic heathen one has as many as nine terms. It has been noted that the more a people are familiar with a thing the more names and technical distinctions they have for it. Following this general rule of thumb it can be seen that our ancestors were much more familiar with the realm of the spirit or psyche than is the Christian doctrine which sought to replace the old traditions. Modern psychology is just now trying to catch up to where our ancestors were centuries ago.

In the midst of the human experience is the human soul. It is that by which we gauge the world and the earth and see them for ourselves. No other area of knowledge has been so wracked by the ravages of the forces of the Christianity than has been our own native "psychology"— or simply put— "teachings about the soul." In ancient times the Germanic peoples had an apparently bewildering number of names for the "soul," "spirit," "mind," and so forth. This is telling in two ways. First, they had many which shows an intimate knowledge of the thing— and also they used these terms in a finely "technical" way without referring to a dogma or psychological school of any kind. It was a deep understanding implicit in the very language used by the folk on an everyday basis.

To recover the lost understandings of the Germanic soul and its workings would be the single greatest key to once and for all requickening the withered roots of the troth. It is probably no accident that serious work in the investigation of the nature of the human soul — divorced from the sometimes superstitious dogmas of the Christians — and the revival of the knowledge of the god of the soul, Odin, began at the same time. Despite the many wrong turns and dead-ends the often misguided investigators have made— there has been some development. Perhaps no other school of modern psychological teaching has been more beneficial than that found by the Swiss psychiatrist Carl Jung.

But what we present here is an attempt to recover the old traditional lore of the soul as it was understood by our ancestors. Here we will also reconstruct, for modern use, a practical native terminology for talking about the "souls." The first step in doing so is the realization that there is not one "soul," but many, and that there is no one word— other than perhaps "self" that encompasses all aspects of the many "souls." The self stands at the center of the souls and can be the stead where all are held together. This is not, however, a natural phenomenon, but rather something for which a man or a woman must *work*. Also, it must be realized that the strong body-soul split so heavily emphasized in Christianity is missing in true soul-lore. We would rather talk of a body-soul-mind complex for a more complete understanding not only of what the parts are, but also how they relate to one another.

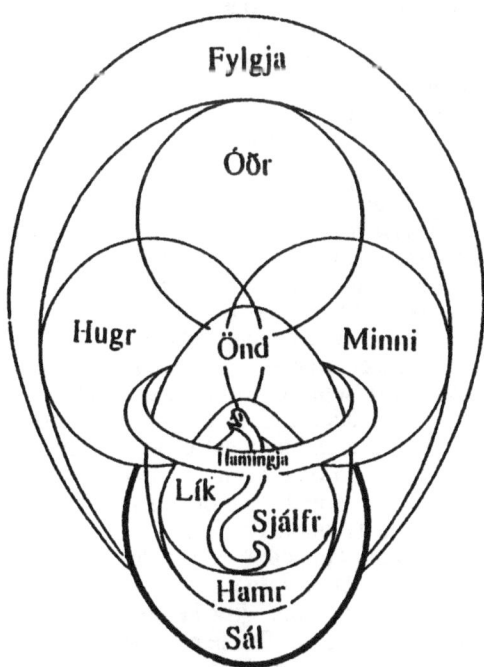

The Traditional Body-Mind Complex

This basic diagram sums up much of the image of the human soul in the traditional sense, although it is by no means exhaustive.

In the very middle we see the self. This is among the most mysterious aspects of the soul, and the least familiar to the everyday experience of many because it is deep within— behind the eye of our soul, as it were. It grows and becomes strong as it is fed by true deeds and profound inner experience. See below for more ideas on this concept.

The lyke (or lich) is the "body." This is the physical vehicle with which most parts of the soul are fused. It is the doorway through which experience is gained and that which allows our wills to have effect. It is not, as others would have you think, an enemy of the spirit, but is indeed its best friend in the whole scheme. For it allows man to exist in Midgard— his true home and the stead where he is best suited to do his work. Behind the body is a sort of mysterious plasmic quasi-material usually having the rough shape of the body itself. This can be called simply the shape or form, or more traditionally the hyde.

The hugh is the intellectual and analytical part of man. The "mind" and the will are embodied in this. Closely allied with this part of the soul is the myne, which is the reflective part of the mind. In the myne is the well of ancestral memories, as well as those personal ones from the individual's own life-time. These two aspects should work in close harmony with one another. The myne provides material of deep an eternal significance for the hugh to work on, and both working together can come to right answers. These soul-aspects are reflected in the ravens of Odin: Huginn and Muninn.

The breath of life is the athem. It keeps the whole being fed with the energies that sustain it in life and "keep the body and soul together."

The other aspects of the should are more mysterious, and are not often directly experienced. This is in contrast to those already discussed which, at least on some low level, we experience every waking moment of the day and through dreams of sleep. Wode is the new English form that we would have for that essential aspect of Wod-en- the power of "inspiration," even "mania" as the Greeks would have called it. Experience of this is extraordinary— it constitutes an "altered state of consciousness." The fetch can be understood in the traditional sense as an entity separate from the individual, but which is attached to him for the duration of his life. It is the conduit through which the gods communicate to him, and the embodiment of all that he has ever been. It is a storehouse of images and powers from beyond this life and from beyond Midgard. It stores up all the experiences of this life in order that it can go on beyond this life to continue its work. The fetch is very rarely experienced in any direct way. For most it only "appears" when death is near— when a man is "fay." The fetch is that which is responsible for the common phenomena of one's life "passing before one's eyes" just before death, or the appearances of spectral female figures at that time. The fetch seen as an entity of the opposite sex of that of the person in question. This can also have a guardian aspect, in which case it can be called the warden. Closely associated with the fetch is the luck of the person. In this is housed all of the echoes of all of the deeds ever done by the bodies to which the fetch has ever been bound. The soul proper is, in the technical sense, the psychic body, or "shade," which embodies the self after the death of the lyke.

Working With Ørlög

The old German *Meister*, Guido von List, exhorts us to work with our fates, not to strive against them. This is sage advice, as no one can really alter the past. It is only from the *present moment* that fate, or *ørlög* can be affected. This is done by practicing the Nine Noble Virtues. Positive fate, or good luck, or good fortune, is the result of *ørlög*— what has been laid down in the past. This past action extends back into previous "incarnations," or embodiments, of your *hamingja* or fetch. This is why fate seems to be so mysterious and inexplicable. In fact it is quite explicable, only its origins are usually entirely *hidden* from us. That is all right, as how negative repercussions originated is not really all that important. What is important is that positive action be taken in the here and now, in the present moment, to begin to alter the effects of negative past action. Positive action is action in accordance and harmony with the Nine Noble Virtues. It is found that action undertaken in a highly conscious way is ten times more potent than actions undertaken in an unconscious, or sleep-walking state. We mainly just sleep-walk through life. That is, our level of awareness as we make our way thought the day is like sleep as compared to the level of awareness that is possible. Therefore the good news is that conscious action can in the time-span of a year overcome the negative, unconscious build-up of ten years.

The Nine Noble virtues are:

> Courage
> Truth
> Honor
> Loyalty
> Discipline
> Hard-Work
> Hospitality
> Self-Reliance
> Perseverance

Courage, also called heartiness, is the bravery to do what is right at all times. This may not always be an act of physical prowess. In fact it may be the courage to tell the truth in a personally disadvantageous circumstance. Truth is the willingness to be honest and say what one knows in one's own heart to be true and right. This is the highest form of morality— not one based on a fear of punishment, but one based on an inner sense of what is right. Honor, which is also called worthiness, is the feeling of inner value and worth from which one knows that one is noble of being, and the desire to show respect for this quality when it is found in the world. It is something that reflects on you in other men's eyes. Fidelity, which is troth, or loyalty, is the unbending will to be loyal to one's gods and goddesses, to one's folk, and to one's own inner self. Loyalty is a virtue unto itself, which gives the one who is loyal great power, even if the thing or person to whom one has given one's loyalty proves to be less perfect than you had imagined. Loyalty is not conditional on how you feel that day. Discipline, or hardiness, is the willingness to be hard with one's self first, and then if need be, with others in order that greater purposes can be achieved. Hospitality, which really boils down to friendliness, is the willingness to share what one has with one's fellows, especially when they are far from home. Industriousness, or basic hard-work, is the willingness to work with maximal effort, and always striving for the highest level of efficiency, as a joyous activity in itself. Self-reliance, which is another way of saying freedom, is the spirit of independence which is striven toward not only for the individual but also for the family, clan, tribe, and nation. Strive to be as self-contained and self-sustaining as possible. Perseverance, or steadfastness, is that spirit of stick-to-itiveness that can always bring one back from defeat or failure— each time we fail we recognize it for what it is, and, if the purpose is true and good, we preserver until success is won.

All true brothers should keep holy the Nine Noble Virtues. How each of these are to be understood is largely a matter of individual reflection and kindred values. In a more traditional world, these Nine Noble Virtues might be spoken to us by our kindly elders as: "Be hearty, forthright, worthy, true, hard, friendly, hard-working, free, and steadfast in all that you undertake." If these values are taught and held by ourselves, for ourselves and our offspring, a solid groundwork will be laid for the rebirth of the troth. All of these values, not just some of them, must be practiced and taught as the Nine Noble Virtues. Too often these values have been passed on under false guises, such as the so-called "Protestant work-ethic," and other such nonsense. These are *our* values made for us, by us, and have nothing whatever to do with the foreign cult. The foreign cult teaches such nonsense as the "forgiveness of sins." Our tradition holds that so sin can be forgiven. Negative, or immoral actions must be overcome with positive, moral and virtuous ones. A crime, even that committed by a god, must be recompensated for. Christianity teaches that a man can escape the consequences of his actions, and thus it actually encourages sin and immorality. Our tradition is far more logical and forthright. There is hope in the Germanic way, however. That hope springs from the idea that highly conscious action, be it ethical or magical, has a higher level of potency than actions committed in a non-conscious state. Most actions of "evil" are ones that are committed in a non-conscious, or low-conscious, state. If you had *known* better, you probably would not have acted in that manner.

Thus fate, or ørlög, can be overcome, but only through the hard-work involved in the exercise of all of the the Nine Noble Virtues, or though the even more arduous and difficult pathway of inner work. It is far more likely that success will follow if the outer path of the Nine Noble virtues is followed as a way of overcoming the effects of ørlög.

Chapter Six

The Holy Stead

Our ancestors were able to make any stead (place) holy wherever they found themselves. When they traveled to new lands, they had a way of "unfolding" the sacred landscape on the new land. This is how Iceland, even though it was only settled by the Norse in the 9th century was *instantly* able to acquire an "ancient" spiritual landscape, Just as whole peoples and tribes can take their sacred spaces with them, so to can individual true folk take their spiritual landscapes with them wherever they find themselves.

You find yourself in a similar situation now. Perhaps your immediate physical surroundings are difficult to see as being "sacred." But it is your mission to sacralize the environment as an act of your own will, and the will of other brothers with whom you now find yourself. This can be done, as it was done in ancient times.

Books are often full of descriptions of special ritual equipment. The fact is that our ancestors often used ordinary objects in the carrying out of sacred work. Often there were special sacred objects, but more often than not it was not the fancy or ornate character of the object that made it sacred, but rather its history: who it had belonged to, and where it had been.

Sacred work can be done with simple objects. If you cannot have a horn, use a paper cup, if you cannot have mead, use water. Other objects can appear to be ordinary, but can be made extraordinary by your repeated use of them and the fact that you have dedicated them to your true work.

If it can be arranged, do not reject the use of the Christian sanctuary or church-space in your facility. The Christians simply took over our own sacred symbols and made them their own— because our ancestors were not about to give up their sacred symbols. So if you have to opportunity to use a Christian space of worship, do so in the spirit that you are taking back what they took from our ancestors centuries ago.

Workings such as the hammer signing or the hammer working can sanctify you and your surroundings wherever you happen to find yourself. This is how our ancestors made any land they might be on at that time a "holy land." The holiness is something we carry inside ourselves and it is something we can virtually *unfold* at any time or place the *need* arises. We have a sacred technology for the unfoldment of the holy wherever we need it.

True Tools

Here we will discuss the types of tools needed for true work. Certain special rites may involve others, but they will be discussed in those places. Here are the basic tools a true brother would need to begin working within a kindred today.

A harrow should be set up upon which all holy is undertaken. This harrow ("altar") may be indoors or outside. Indoor harrows (also called "stalls") are usually made of wood (tables or shelves are most often used), and are ideally at least two feet by two feet, but any dimension will do. It is much better that this object is used for holy work *only*.

On the harrow or stall there will usually be four items: 1) the horn (or cup), 2) the blessing bowl, 3) the evergreen tine (twig), and 4) the vessel for the holy liquid arranged as shown.

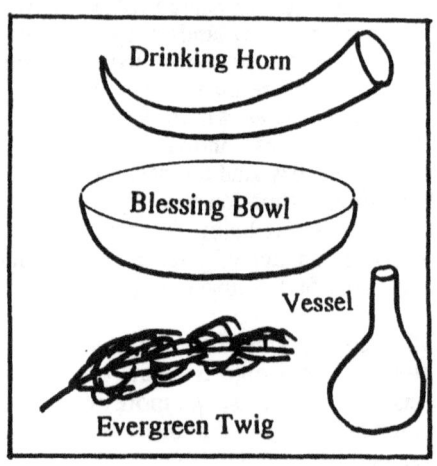

The Stall Arrangement

The horn is a very traditional vessel from which to drink the holy drought during the working of the blessing. Ceremonial cups or chalices can also be used, however. A paper cup can also be used, if necessary.

The blessing bowl should ideally be made of wood, and should be large enough that it will hold approximately half of the contents of the horn or cup being used. For indoor rites there is also an auxiliary bowl which is placed on the floor to the (western) side of the stall. This auxiliary bowl will receive the outpouring of the liquid, which in outdoor ceremonies would be poured out onto the ground. The contents of this other bowl are then solemnly poured out onto the ground outside after the conclusion of the working.

The tine or evergreen twig is to be cut from some conifer tree or bush for every blessing. It is normally placed on the ground (or in the auxiliary bowl) and marks the spot where the final outpouring of the sanctified liquid is to take place. It is, of course, primarily used as a tool with which to sprinkle the harrow and kindred with the holy liquid— to do the blessing itself.

The vessel containing the liquid to be used in the blessing should be a special one. It will be used to the holy liquid into the horn, before it is circulated and hallowed. This vessel is usually an earthenware bottle or jar.

These are the basic tools for the rites known as "blessings," or *blótar* in Old Norse.

Chapter Seven

The Rites

The nature of the rites of the troth, or of Ásatrú or Odinism, is that of giving gifts to the gods and receiving their gifts in return to us. The gods generally share most of their blessing with us regardless of whether we repay them or not. But he who takes their gifts without acknowledging and repaying them is really a thief. No good can come from stealing from the gods!

The troth of the ancestors does not require that the one officiating in the rituals be some kind of "ordained priest." As a folk religion, the troth allows for any man who considers himself to be true, that is loyal to the old gods of his ancestors, to officiate at such rites. The kindred leader should be someone who has considerable knowledge about the religion and the culture, but who is also a strong leader in ritual.

The rituals forge bonds— they bond the individual to the gods and the folk-group to one another and to the gods. This is the essence of gift-giving and this is the nature of how the blessings function in the religious life of true folk.

Common Procedures in Ritual Work

In the texts of the rites presented below there are, as in all rites involving deep traditions, many elements that will be repeated. These are elements that give a timeless and traditional orientation to much of what is done. We will speak about these elements here in some detail, so that we will not have to repeat them over and over, and so that they can be presented in a clear and understandable manner. It is in the right and true understanding and doing of some of these traditional elements that great power can be poured into the work.

Besides this, we will present the basic structural formulas of the blessing, from which individual true brothers can construct their own rites in an authentic and traditional manner. This kind of formulaic outline is the true essence of the Germanic tradition— basic continuity with the ever-present possibility of creative innovation. However, you should stick tot he basic patterns or ritual formula outlined here.

The basic formula of the blessing (or *blót*) follows a nine-fold plan:

Name	Function
1) Hallowing	sets ritual space/time apart from ordinary
2) Reading	puts rite into mythic context
3) Rede	links myth or the purpose of the rite
4) Call	invokes deities or classes of beings
5) Loading	charges drink with godly power
6) Drinking	circulates godly power within
7) Blessing	circulates godly power without
8) Giving	returns rightful part of power to divinity
9) Leaving	declares work rightly done/return to ordinary

All workings outlined in this book can be performed with a single celebrant, who is always designated with the term "speaker" in the texts. However, in kindred settings it is usually best if several persons take an active part in the working of the rite. The roles can be divided as the kindred leader sees fit. The most traditional type of division of work would be into three roles, called 1) theal, 2) shope, and 3) goodman. The theal is responsible for all speaking parts that involve calling on the divine powers and distributing their blessings. The shope is responsible for all speaking parts involving the setting of mythic and social context. The goodman is responsible for all of the non-speaking ritual actions having to do with the actual distribution of the holy liquid. A modification of this use is for the goodman to take the speaking roles. Allowing the theal to undertake the ritual actions of distributing the holy liquid. These are, however, only suggestions. Any permutation of these roles can be practiced.

In the beginning of some workings the speaker is instructed to strike the holy posture indicated by the *madr*-rune. To do this one simply stands straight with the arms straight out and up at an approximately forty-five degree angle, simulating the runestave shape of the younger m-rune. This is an ancient pose used by the Germanic peoples when coming into communication with the gods and goddesses; it was even noted by the Romans.

The Hammer-Working

The normal way to hallow a stead, or sanctify a place, for holy work is by means of the hammer-working. This sets the place apart from the outside, everyday, profane world, making it special and outside ordinary time/space. In this especially prepared space/time holy work can be rightly done. It should be noted that if you have a permanent holy stead, which is never used for any thing other than holy activities, then such a place is called permanently holy, or sacrosanct. In such a case the hammer-working is unnecessary.

To perform the hammer-working one faces north and makes the sing of the hammer [_⊥_] by tracing it in the air, imagining it be drawn in space, hovering in the air to the north of the holy site. While doing this the speaker says: "Hammer in the north! Hold and hallow this stead!" this process is repeated in the east, south, and west. Then the speaker returns to the north and looks upward, tracing the hammer sign high above the ritual site, and says: "Hammer above me [or us]! Hold and hallow this stead!" then the speaker looks below and again makes the sign, visualizing it deep below the ritual site, and says: "Hammer below me [or us]! Hold and hallow this stead!" Thus the site is surrounded by six hammer signs. These will guard the stead from disturbing forces, but will make it attractive and hospitable to the gods, goddesses, and all other friendly wights.

The Holy Calendar

The ancient Germanic year was divided first into two main halves: Winter and Summer. The whole was then subdivided into eight parts. We continue that practice today. Although there are generally eight holy steads in time in the ritual calendar, they are not all equal in importance. It was customary in ancient times to designate three times as being most holy. These three often varied from tribe to tribe. Of universal importance was, however, the Yule-Tide. Other important times were Midsummer, Spring (Easter), or the Harvest-Tide in the fall.

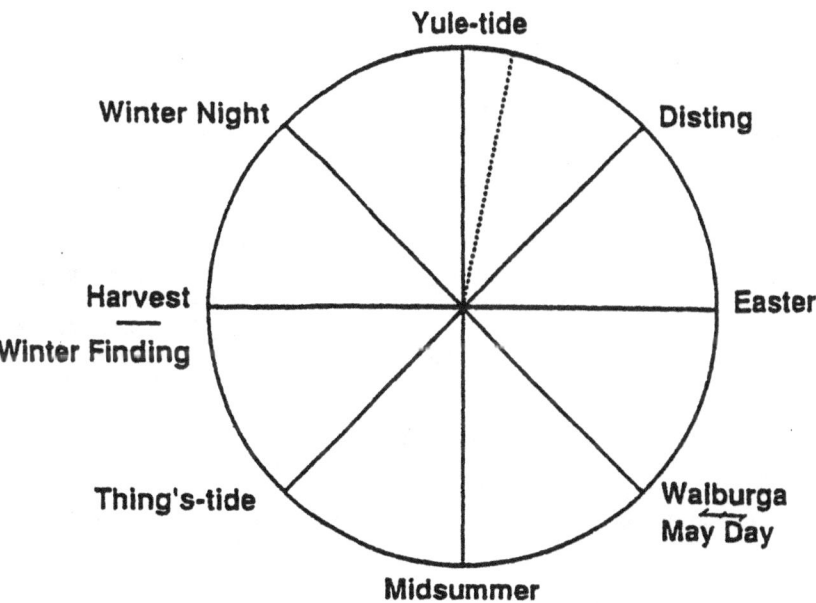

The Eightfold Division of the Year

Besides these seasonal rites, it can now become customary to have weekly meetings of a religious nature. These help remind us of our troth and also act as educational opportunities.

Daily Rites
Besides the seasonal rites, there are daily rites or devotions that the true man, or true brother, can observe. These are:

Morning Work (from rising to about 10 o'clock)
Noontide Work (sometime between 11:00 and 1:00)
Evening Work (just before or after sundown)
Night Work (anytime after three hours after sundown)

The Morning Work consists of donning the Hammer and reciting "Sigrdrifumal" 3-4— the text of which can be found in the *Poetic Edda*. Shortly after you rise in the morning, and before you have undertaken anything of significance, ritually put on your Thorr's hammer amulet or token. (It can be any sort of Thorr's Hammer.) If you wear the hammer at all times, even when you sleep, it should be removed, and replaced around your neck with the words:

"Now I don the Hammer of Thorr, may it lead me in right ways,
against all wrong ways of the giants."

Other words can be substituted. The important thing is to take off and replace the hammer anew on a daily basis, and focus on the idea that the hammer will guide and lead you in the right ways throughout the day. After this perform the Hammer-Sign:

Work of the Hammer-Sign

In this work, true folk can reach up into the holy light and might of the gods and make it a part of themselves. To begin, the person should visualize a bright shining ball of golden light two or three feet above the head. Then with the right hand reach up into that light and make a fist, grasping the light-substance in the hand, which should then be drawn down tot eh forehead. Touch your forehead and says: "Tyr!" then continue to pull the light down through the head and touch the mouth and say: "Odin!" Next draw the light down in a column through the body and touch the solar plexus and say: "Thorr!" then move the fist, and the light contained in it, from the solar plexus to the left shoulder; touch the shoulder and say: "Freyr!" Now, drawing light across the body in a horizontal direction, touch the light to the right shoulder and say: "Freyja!"

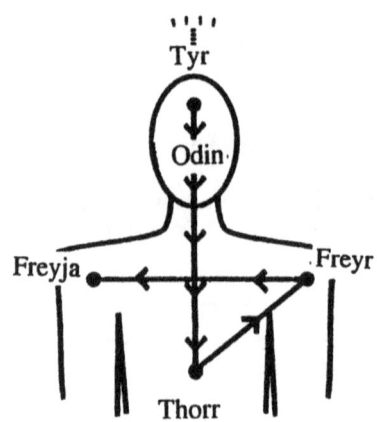

The Hammer-Sign in the Body

The Great Blessings of Ásatrú

(1) The Great Blessing of the Winter Nights
(Mid-October)

The Blessing of the Dises
The stall is to be set up in the usual manner.

1. Hallowing
The hammer-working is wrought to ward the stead and make it holy, after which the speaker says:

"Thus this stead is hallowed for our work here tonight. As the god Heimdall wards the Bifrost Bridge, so this stead is warded against all unholy wights and ways."

2. Reading
The "Völuspá" from the *Poetic Edda*.

3. Rede
The speaker, in the [+]-posture, says:

"Hail ye holy ides   dises of the stall,
    hold ye whole the kindred:
mighty mothers of old   turn our minds toward you!
    wend ye neigh these winter nights!"

4. Call
The speaker lowers his arms, turns to the gathered folk and says:

"Tonight we name the Winter Night and call forth the dises of the kindred. Ye have been known by many names, ye great mothers of our folk who ever drive us forward to more daring deeds, and to more fruitful fields—
O, ye spae-ides, ye wondrous womanly wights all-weird, we call you:
    Jódís of the horse,
    Hjórdís of the sword,
    Valdís of the fallen,
    Vígdís of battle,
    Ásdís of the Æsir,
    Irmundís of the fight,
    Herdís of the host!"

5. Loading
Again turn to face the stall (to the north), the speaker pours drink into the horn or other drinking vessel, and holds it aloft, saying:
"We give this drink, blended with awe, to you O mighty mothers all-old!"

6. Drinking
The horn is then individually handed to each true man gathered before the stall. The folk are to drink half of the contents of the horn, and the speaker is to return the undrunk part of the drink to the stall, where it is poured into the blessing bowl. As each true man is handed the horn, he makes the hammer-sign over its rim, and may speak a spell from the heart on the coming year.

7. Blessing
Once the process of handing the horn around is complete, the speaker stands before the stall and makes the sign of the hammer ⊥ over the center of the blessing bowl, while intoning the holy words:

"This drink is hallowed to the dises of the kindred and of the folk."

The speaker then circles the stall three times with the sun, all the while sprinkling the stall itself with the liquid from the evergreen bough. While doing this he should say:

"To all the dead dises and to all the awesome ides!"

Then the speaker should the members of the kindred, then all the known good folk and true.

8. Giving
The speaker now removes the blessing bowl from the stall, takes it to a point just north of the stall, and pours its contents out into a bowl with the words:

"Holy mothers of men,   holy mothers of women,
     awesome daughters of Odin,
     to you we give this drink!"

9. Leaving
Again the speaker returns to his original place before the stall, faces northward with arms aloft and says:

"From these nights to the Twelfth Night of Yule, the walls between the worlds of the dises all-dead, and of us all-living here, grow ever thinner— may the wisdom of these weird women, all-loving, become known all here tonight! Let us now go forth and make merry, for the year is young!"

The Blessing of the Elves
In addition to the Blessings of the Dises, a Blessing of the Elves can also be performed on the Winter Nights. The procedure is identical to that of the Blessing of the Dises; however, the speeches in points 3), 4), 5) 8), and 9) should read as follows:

3) "Hail the holy Elves, shining of the stall,
    whole ye hold the kindred,
  mighty elders of old turn our minds toward you!"

4) "Tonight we name the Winter Night and call forth the elder elves of the kindred. Ye have been known by many names, ye great elders of our folk who ever lead us to greater lore, and fare us to more fruitful fields.
O, ye Light-elves above and ye Dark-elves down under— we call you! Fare ye forth from the realm of light upon the ray of the elves— stream to us from on high! Fare ye forth from the realm of darkness upon the ray of elves— stream to us stream to us from down under!"

5) "We give this drink, blended with awe, to you wondrous wights of the land and airs, to you awesome elves all-old!"

7) "This drink is hallowed to the elves of the kindred!'

"To all the awesome elves, to those who dwell in darkness,
    and to those who live in light!"

8) "All ye elves of the eleven realms, awesome elders all,
    weird land-wights,
    to you we give this drink!"

9) "From these nights to the Twelfth Night of Yule, the walls between the worlds of those dark-elves and the light, and our world here, grow ever thinner— the lore of light and the dreams of darkness are becoming ever more known to us throughout this tide! Let us now go forth and be glad, for the year is yet but young!"

(2) The Great Blessing of the Yule-Tide
(December 20-31)

The Yule-Tide is a complex blessing. Ideally it should be celebrated over the twelve nights between the Mother Night and the Twelfth Night (Yule proper). During this time there should be general celebration among the kindred. However, our modern world usually makes much of this impossible. Since twelve nights of the Yule-Tide represent the whole year, certain workings of galdor and divination can also be effectively undertaken during this time. It is fitting to read through the entire *Poetic Edda*, preferably out loud before the gathered folk in the evenings, during the twelve nights of the Yule-Tide.

Mother-Night: Beginning of the Yule-Tide
(December 20)

On the Mother-Night an all-around blessing is to be held, which will ritually be answered by the all-around blessing held at Midsummer. After the blessing the gathered folk will partake of the most important symbol of the year— the symbol of the Yule-Tide, at which time the ancestors are naturally closest to us, the living.

The All-Around Blessing of the Mother-Night

The stall is set up in the standard fashion.

1. Hallowing
The hammer-working is performed, at the conclusion of which the speaker says:

"This stead is hallowed for our work here tonight. As the god Heimdall wards the Bifrost Bridge, so this stead is warded against all unholy wights and ways."

2. Reading (Lay)
The "Völuspá" and/or the "Lay of Helgi Hjörvarðsson" and the other "Helgi lays" are to be read or recited to the gathered folk.

3. Rede
The speaker says:
"This mid-night upon the Mother-Night we gather as in nights of yore, to greet the sun at her lowest stead, and to honor all the gods and goddesses who swell in Asgard, and all our own forebears who dwell in the halls of Hárr and Hel. We call upon them to make ripe their might and main in our lives. We call upon them all — the holy gathering — living as a whole as is Odin's Law."

4. Call
The speaker makes the following calls. After each call, the gathered folk give welcome to the god or goddess being called with their name, and the words: "We Give Thee Welcome!"

> "Odin, we are awed by thy craft,
> Tyr, we stay true to three forever,
> Balder, thy brightness and boldness guides us,
> Frigga, thy fruit and wisdom keeps us all,
> Idunna, thine apples strengthen our souls,
> Thor, thy thunder wards our stead,
> Freyja, we get freedom from thy frolic,
> Freyr, from thee we get a harvest of frith."

Then a litany of divine attributes of the gods and goddesses just called is recited by the speaker. After each the gathered folk shout: "We give thee welcome!"

"Rune-Lord,
One-Handed God,
Holder of the Hringhorn,
Lady of the gods and goddesses,
Keeper of the apples,
Guardian of Asgard,
Holder of the Brisingamen,
God of the Wain."

"Again we all to you in all your names, be among us here this mid-night as the year reaches its depth and Sunna stands sunken to her lowest stead:

Hail all the gods,   hail all the goddesses,
    Hail all thy holy ones
    Who dwell together."

5. Loading
The speaker pours drink into he horn and says:

"We give you the gifts of our works woven and blended with the might and main of this drink. It lends us — gods and folk together — help in our striving toward the shining plain where the worlds and wights dwell in wholeness. The year has come into its depth of darkness— the serpent slithers among the deepest roots of the World-Tree— may his sight find us not wanting in wisdom."

6. Drinking
The speaker then drinks from the horn and pours the remainder into the blessing bowl on the stall. The horn is then refilled and passed to each of the gathered folk. Each makes the sign of the hammer over the rim of the horn before drinking. Each time the remainder of the drink is poured into the blessing bowl by the speaker.

7. Blessing
The speaker now sprinkles the stall and the gathered folk with the words:

"The blessings of all the gods and goddesses of our folk be upon us!"

8 Giving
After the blessing is completed, the speaker pours the contents of the blessing bowl out into a bowl to the east of the stall with the words:

"To Odin, Tyr, Balder, Frigga, Idunna, Thor, Freyja, Freyr and to all the gods and goddesses of our folk: for good growth among folk and upon the land!"

9. Leaving
The speaker returns to the stall and says:

"Thus the work is once again wrought, it renews our hearts to do worthy deeds, and to strive toward our goals with mighty moods, wise words, and trust in our own might and main— ever holding to our oaths to ourselves and to our folk!"

Twelfth Night: The Festival of Yule
(December 31)

This is the culmination of the Yule-Tide, and religiously the most important of the twelve nights of Yule. The rebirth of the Sun is completed on this night. In the deep tradition of the Yule-oath the origins of our "New Year's resolutions" are to be found.

You should make a traditional Yule-wreath, which is a wreath with sticks through the center to from a solar cross:

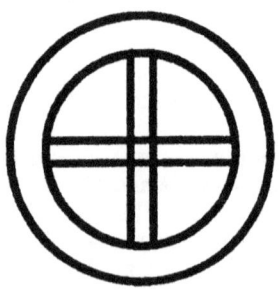

Yule-Wreath

The Yule-wreath is then placed in the middle of the stall for the working.

1. Hallowing
The stead is hallowed with the hammer working, at the conclusion of which a ring is drawn on the ground around the gathered folk.

2. Call
The officiating speaker stands before the stall, facing the north in the m-rune posture, and says:

"By the bristles of the boar!
Jólnir (Odin) lord of the Yule-Tide
We call upon thee to witness
These our oaths of Yule
Jólaheit skaltu heyra ok heit skullum vér strengja!"
[yoh-la-hayt skaltoo hayra ok hayt skullum ver streng-ya]
(Thou shalt hear the oaths of Yule and we shall bind the oaths.)

3. Oath Taking
Each of the gathered true brothers then steps up to the stall and with the right hand grasps the center of the Yule-wreath. With the left hand this individual lifts the horn aloft and speaks his own personal oath or boast. After the speech is through, he drinks half of the contents of the horn and pours the rest out as a gift with the words:

"To Jólnir and to the oaths of Yule!"

As each person finishes, the officiating speaker refills the horn for the next one. This is repeated until all oaths are taken.

4. Blessing of the Yule-Wreath
The speaker then takes up position before the stall and lays his hands upon the middle of the wreath and speaks these words:

"Jólnir, ruling the Yule-Tide,
We yearn for thy might,
Yare the year in the yard to make!
In the year of this Yule
Are we tried and true:
We plight our troth
And truly pledge
To hold these holy oaths
In the year of the Yule!"

The speaker then once more stands in the m-rune position and says:

"Jólnir, ruling the Yule-Tide,
We yearn for thy might—
That when the yarn of the year is yielded
yare the year in the yard was made!"

The gathered folk then meditate deeply on the wreath and its significance as a sign of the sun, carrying their oaths aloft.

5. Leaving
No formal closing is used here, as the purpose of the rite is the opening of the whole year to the holy power in the year to come. Each retreats in his own time back to the main gathering area.

It is of extreme importance that the wreath now be disposed of in a dignified manner— preferably by *burning*.

(3) The Great Blessing of Disting
(Around February 14)

Disting is a festival of importance to the home region. It is given to the dises (from whom it gets its name), and thus it is strongly linked to the Winter Nights festival. But it is really given more for gatherings of a social and/or clanic nature, and traditionally at a time when local Things are held. At this time, the Earth is prepared to have the seeds sown so that growth will take place in the land.

Also, gifts may be given to the dises and elves at this time. But the tide is really most holy to the goddess Freyja and to the god Váli. It is the right time to do the Blessing of Váli, the god of vengeance, and thus of rebirth.

Blessing of Váli

For this working a piece of thread about a foot long is needed.

1. Hallowing
Perform the hammer-working.

2. Reading
Read or recite the "Short Seeress Prophecy" from the *Poetic Edda*.

3. Rede
"On this day/night we remember the ties of kin, and understand our bonds with them. We remember as well our kindred oaths of troth and trust to the siblings gathered around the stall."

4. Call
"Váli, son of Rind, the Etin-wife now among the Æsir— and Sigtyr, son of Borr, born of Buri, spawn of the wind-cold corn!"

5. Loading
Drink is poured into the horn. An assistant to the speaker stands with the twine held in a loose knot over the rim of the horn, as the speaker says:

"Dweller in the homesteads of the forebears— thou art the god who frees long-bound force! Unbind now the bond of narrow blindness— free us from the fetters in which we have long abode, apart from kith and kindred! Unbind the bonds and free the fetters— as the knot is un-knit. . . (here the knot over the rim of the horn is unknoted). . . boundless are the bonds, free the fetters! Váli-Áli-Váli-Áli-Váli— god of vengeance— heave up the holy might of the old ones, who rest unquietly deep down below! Rebind us in their troth, again we hear their holy Rede, and with this knot we again know their mighty myne."

(Here the assistant ties the twine onto the horn.)

>   "Váli to thee vows   and valued oaths
>   are gladly given   all great gifts:
>   lift the elders' lives in love bind the kin
>   in homes 'round holy hearths."

(Speaker hallows the horn with the hammer-sign.)

6. Drinking
The horn is passed around for each to hallow and drink from, and is returned to the speaker, who pours the remainder into the blessing bowl with the formula:

>   "Váli-Áli-Váli-Áli-Váli!"

7. Blessing
The holy liquid is sprinkled on the stall and on the gathered folk with the words:

"May the blessings of Váli be upon this stall and upon the gathered folk."

8. Giving
The holy liquid is poured out onto the ground to the west of the stall with the words:

"To Váli, and to Freyja, is this gift given!"

9. Leaving
"By the wonder of Odin, by the troth of Tyr, and by the thunder of Thor— so shall it be!"

(4) The Great Blessing of Easter (Ostara)
Spring Equinox
(Around March 21)

The stall is fitted out with a horn, vessel holding drink, blessing bowl, bough of evergreen, and three candles (black, red, and white), arranged in the following manner:

White

      Black   Red

1. Hallowing
The hammer-working is performed.
The speaker faces the sunrise in the east in the m-rune posture and says:
"This stead is hallowed to our work here this morning. As the god Heimdall wards the Bifrost Bridge, so the stead is warded against all unholy wights and ways."

After a pause the speaker continues:

"Hail holy Easter! Hail the daughter born at Delling's Door, at the Gate of Day who bears the light! hail Easter, lady of the dawn!"

2. Reading
Here the "Sigrdrífumál" from the *Poetic Edda* is read or recited.

3. Rede
Still facing east, the speaker says:

"This morning we are gathered to call forth the mighty lady of the new-born light. Warded by the steeds of heaven, she rises and gives us light, love, and lust, and she bears also an awesome side, middling and mighty. This our foes shall doom, yet we too must know it well and love it well for to wax great in wisdom."

4. Call
Speaker stands to the west of the stall, facing east, and salutes the east with the words:

"Easter, we raise the sign of the sword in thy honor, come and dwell among the folk of the sax! In the dawn, we see thy birth, in the day we know thy power, and in the dusk we trust that thou shalt turn back to us full well soon."

Speaker then replaces the sword on the stall and continues:

"No mask has hidden thy holy name from us, and now we call thee forth by deeds right and holy:
Easter— drottning of the dawn, queen of heaven— clothed in white and gold — break now forth in all thy might, let us know thy main!"

The speaker now lights the three candles on the altar in the order: white red, black. As he lights them, the following is spoken:

"We now kindle thee three-fold fire of spring, in this new dawn of the year we start the fire of its birth (white candle is lit), we light the flame of its life (red candle is lit), and we kindle the lamp of its death (black candle is lit)— as signs of the timeless, ever-becoming power of our souls.

5. Loading
Speaker pours drink into the horn and holds it aloft with the words:

"To thee, awesome Easter, who knows the ways of Odin, we give to thee the gifts of our works all woven and blended with the might of this drink. As we lend you this drink, so lend us thy might— haunt our hearts, abide in our breaths, make whole our minds and mighty our moods and memories!
Hail Easter!
Hail the awesome Ostara!, Ostara! Ostara!

6. Drinking
The horn is then passed among the gathered folk and the remainder is poured into the blessing bowl on the stall by the speaker.

7. Blessing
The speaker then goes on the sprinkle first the stall (tuning around it three times with the sun), and then all the good folk and true. While doing this the speaker repeats at will:

"The blessings of Easter upon us!"

8. Giving
The speaker then pours out the contents of the blessing bowl to the east of the stall with the words:

"To Easter we give this gift!"

9. Leaving
The blessing bowl is returned to the stall, the speaker faces the new dawn and says:

"Thus the work of wonder is wrought! The fires of spring burn, the power of Easter burns forth, she blooms in our minds, and we move with her might. We know her blessings all the year through!"

At the conclusion of the working it is traditional to leap up in the air as high as you can three times.

(5) The Great Blessing of Midsummer
(June 21)

This is one of the three Great Blessings of the troth, at which gifts are given to all of the gods and goddesses of the troth in common. The celebration of these three blessings, the other two being Yule and Harvest, are the essential acts of good and true brothers.
The stall is set up in the standard fashion.

1. Hallowing
The hammer-working is performed, that conclusion of which the speaker says:

"This stead is hallowed for our work here today. As the god Heimdall wards the Bifrost Bridge, so this stead is warded against all unholy wights and ways."

2. Reading
The lay of "Baldr's Dreams" from the *Poetic Edda* is read or recited to the gathered folk.

3. Rede
The speaker says:

"This noon-tide of the Midsummer we gather together as in days of yore, to greet the Sun at her highest stead, and to honor all the gods and goddesses who dwell in Asgard. We call upon them to make ripe their might and main in our lives. We call upon them all — the holy many — living as a whole, as is Odin's Law."

4. Call
The speaker makes the following calls. After each call, the gathered folk give welcome to the god or goddess being called with their name, and the words: "We Give Thee Welcome!"

"Odin, we are awed by thy craft,
Tyr, we stay true to three forever,
Balder, thy brightness and boldness guides us,
Frigga, thy fruit and wisdom keeps us all,
Idunna, thine apples strengthen our souls,
Thor, thy thunder wards our stead,
Freyja, we get freedom from thy frolic,
Freyr, from thee we get a harvest of frith."

Then a litany of divine attributes of the gods and goddesses just called is recited by the speaker. After each the gathered folk shout: "We give thee welcome!"

"Rune-Lord,
One-Handed God,
Holder of the Hringhorn,
Lady of the gods and goddesses,
Keeper of the apples,
Guardian of Asgard,
Holder of the Brisingamen,
God of the Wain."

"Again we all to you in all your names, be among us here this mid-night as the year reaches its depth and Sunna stands sunken to her lowest stead:

> Hail all the gods,   hail all the goddesses,
>   hail all thy holy ones
>   who dwell together."

5. Loading
The speaker pours drink into the horn and says:

"We give you the gifts of our works woven and blended with the might and main of this drink. It lends us — gods and folk together — help in our striving toward the shining plain where the worlds and wights dwell in wholeness. The year has come to its peak of power— the eagle gazes from the topmost branch of the World-Tree— may his sight find us not wanting in wisdom."

6. Drinking
The speaker then drinks from the horn and pours the remainder into the blessing bowl on the stall. The horn is then refilled and passed to each of the gathered folk. Each makes the sign of the hammer over the rim of the horn before drinking. Each time the remainder of the drink is poured into the blessing bowl by the speaker.

7. Blessing
The speaker now sprinkles the stall and the gathered folk with the words:

"The blessings of all the gods and goddesses of our folk be upon us!"

8 Giving
After the blessing is completed, the speaker pours the contents of the blessing bowl out into a bowl to the east of the stall with the words:

"To Odin, Tyr, Balder, Frigga, Idunna, Thor, Freyja, Freyr and to all the gods and goddesses of our folk: for good harvest and frith!"

9. Leaving
The speaker returns to the stall and says:

"Thus the work is once again wrought, it renews our hearts to do worthy deeds, and to strive toward our goals with mighty moods, wise words, and trust in our own might and main— ever holding to our oaths to ourselves and to our folk!"

A Blessing of Tyr

1. Hallowing
The hammer-working is done and then the speaker says:

"This thing-stead is hallowed for our work here al these days and nights. By the hammer of Thor is it warded against all that would work ill against us. May we meet in frith and take our leave in grith."

2. Reading
The section of the *Prose Edda* dealing with the loss of Tyr's hand to the Fenris-Wolf is read or recited.

3. Rede
"Under the might and main of the great god Tyr, we are gathered together here, gods and folk together, to hold a holy thing. May he make our moods all-mighty and our words all-wise."

4. Call
"From thy stead deep within the Irminsul we call to thee O mighty lord of laws and leavings of the wolf! Thou who, by the ordeal of battle, metes out good speed and bad, in the highest of laws all-whole. Fare now forth, O mighty one-handed god from thy high-seat deep within the most hidden halls of Asgard! Come shine thy light of law and right over our deeds and doings upon this thing-stead!"

5. Loading
The speaker pours drink into the horn, lifts it aloft and says:

"We give you this horn blended with the might and main of all our deeds and doings, that thou shalt mete out that law as we all have it coming to us! Tyr! Tyr!"

6. Drinking
The speaker makes the sign of the hammer over the rim of the horn, drinks from it, and passes it around to the gathered folk; all make the sign of the hammer or that of the T-rune before drinking. The remainder of the drink in the horn is poured into the blessing bowl on the stall.

7. Blessing
The speaker turns twice around the stall, sprinkling it with the drink, while saying:

"The great blessing of Tyr be upon this thing-stead!"

Then the speaker sprinkles the gathered folk, saying:
"And may his blessing be upon all the gathered folk!"

8. Giving
The blessing bowl is poured out to the north of the stall with the words:

"To Tyr, high-god of the heavens, and to Earth, mother of us all!"

9. Leaving
"Thus our work is wrought. Let us now go forth and speak with wise words, make law with mighty moods, hold hard to our oaths of troth and fellowship, and make merry in frith and grith!"

Chapter Eight

Kindreds

The troth, or Ásatrú, can be practiced by a single, solitary man. Religion is about making bonds, or connections. The Latin word *re-ligio*, from which "religion" is derived, means literally "reconnection." Our ancestors knew this concept well also. The rites and customs of the faith were designed to forge links, or bonds, between and among humans and gods, and in turn between and among humans of the family, clan and tribe. It is therefore also true that the relationship of humans to gods is mirrored in the relationship of men to each other.

These relationships are characterized by the mutual recognition of the Nine Noble Virtues. Gods and men have a mutual contract between themselves, as do, in the best of worlds, human beings. In the absence of organic families, when men find themselves in hostile territory, they band together for support. In the terminology of current Ásatrú these groups are called "kindreds." In the earliest days of the the old AFA (Ásatrú Free Assembly, now the Ásatrú Folk Assembly) these groups were aptly referred to as *skeppslags*. This word literally means "ship's-crew." when a group of men is at sea, on the hostile waves and engaged in a common undertaking, they must band together in order to thrive and survive. These bonds are forged not by brute strength— for if they are they are soon doomed to failure. A group, to be effective and true, must be made up of three levels of hierarchy. These levels are mirrored in the society of the gods themselves. The first level is the leadership level. Leadership must be characterized by moral will, intelligence and inspiration. The leader must know the lore and be knowledgeable about the world and how it works as well. The second level is characterized by strength, physical and moral. The third level is involved with the work of producing things: art, tools, and so on.

A kindred, or any group, must partake of this hierarchy to be really "in tune" with the divine order. To allow strength to dominate intelligence, or to allow production to govern and direct strength is immoral and ungodly. This misuse of the functions, or literally **mal-functions**, far too much characterize our modern society.

As a practical matter, you need to determine what your institution will allow and support in the way of religious organizations. Get your religion certified as legitimate in the eyes of the officials. (A standard form-letter can be issued from Woodharrow to local prison officials certifying Ásatrú as a legitimate religion. To get this document, you must provide the full address of the prison official to whom the letter is to be directed.) Do not allow the prison to say that the Muslims can meet but you cannot. If no one is allowed to have religious groups, that's one thing, but if others are allowed to do it, so should you. In general it is a well-established constitutional right for all humans to be able to practice their religion.

Once you have established your right to form a kindred, or if you have already done so, it should be provided with a set of traditions, you can call them "rules," but indeed they should be more in the spirit of **traditions**. The traditions of the kindred are things which will transcend the individuals in it and make the organization of the kindred go beyond the strict time/space constraints that it appears to have. Traditions involve specific language used in the blessing-formulas that the kindred has created, symbolic objects used in the blessings, and whatever else both: 1) connect your kindred to all others, ancient and modern, and 2) make your kindred something special and set apart from all others that have ever existed, or that will ever exist.

Kindreds should meet on a regular basis: preferably at least once a week. Blessings do not need to be held as a part of a weekly "service," although there is nothing wrong with this, especially as you are learning the mechanics of the rituals. A meeting should consist of a discussion of some aspect of the lore, mythology, and so on, and also perhaps have a discussion of personal goals and accomplishments. This latter function can best be fulfilled in the form of a symbol.

The symbol is a special holy working in its own right, and deserves a good deal of attention from those who wish to work truly. (The word symbol is derived from the Icelandic *sumbl* and the Old English *symbel*, meaning a solemn religious drinking ritual or ritual feast.) It is a coming together of the folk for partaking in the godly drink.

As the great blessings are a way to "bring the divine into the world," the symbol is a way to "maintain the stream of continuity from gods to men and through the generations of time." The symbol keeps the gods and heroes, including our own ancestors, alive and living among us. It is also that time for ritual boasts or oaths. These boasts are not only "bragging" about past accomplishments but also oaths concerning what one is to do in the time to come. They are a way of ritually and objectively putting before one's brothers what one intends to do. In the whole context of the symbol, one swears before the gods and goddesses, before one's brothers. Oaths sworn in this setting have great power, a power derived from many levels and sources.

The formula of the symbol follows a sixfold plan:

Name	Function
1) Seating	puts folk in right/holy order
2) Bringing of Horn	brings holy liquid into the hall
3) Beginning	invokes the purpose of the symbol
4) First Boasts	honors the gods and heroes
5) Other Boasts	works for individuals or groups
6) Leaving	closes rounds

In a symbol, the gathered brothers seat themselves in some significant manner or order. In nights of yore the head of the clan or chieftain would sit at the head of the table or on a high-seat, with those of highest authority immediately below him. Those of less authority, or the younger members of the kindred, would be seated further away from the head. Each kindred will probably have its own system, but it is ritually important to have some tradition in this regard as it increases the level of significance in the arrangement or context in which the actions will take place. After all have taken their seats, a designated person will ceremonially bring in the first horn or cup of holy liquid and set it down before the leader. The leader/speaker then stands up and utters a formal opening to the symbol, such as: "We are rightly gathered. Now we wend our way into the timeless realm unseen, and share together in elder pathways to might and main." Following upon this there is a series of formalized "boasts" (actually drinks to honor the gods and ancestors). Of these we have some remnants directly from Old Norse sources. Such boasts should be drunk at least to Odin, Tyr, Thorr, Freyr and Freyja, followed by general rounds honoring the forebears. Such a series of formalized boasts could be:

1) "To Odin for good speed and wisdom!"
2) "To Tyr for wit and good troth!"
3) "To Thorr for ward and thew!" (= strength)
4) "To Freyr for feast and frith!"
5) "To Freyja for freedom and frolic!"
6) "To our kinsmen whom we ken not, and to those beloved who are buried and burned [here repeat the names of dead relatives, etc.]!"

After the formalized boasts have been completed, there begins an unlimited series of individualized boasts and/or oaths. Each individual may use his or her own horn in drinking the rounds. The nature of these individualized boasts varies from person to person. Some will recount great mythic events, or offer historical events with heroic dimensions of work in skaldic form; while still others will make personal boasts (oaths) concerning things which they intend to bring about in the days to come.

When all have finished the rounds they have planned, and all wode (inspiration) is spent, the rounds are called to a halt by the leader/speaker with a formal declaration, such as: "I call the rounds ended. Let us wend our way back to our stead, back to our time, and go forth from here with mighty moods."

The function of the symbel is is this: It provides a way for kindred members to enter into a holy state and commune with the divine, and at the same time for the kindred members to be able to relate to each other on a higher, more honorable and sacred way. It is a model for inter-human communication that has been used by psychologists and leaders of industry in modern times to great effect.

Kindreds are both study groups and groups formed for the purpose of celebrating the holy blessings of the religion. A byproduct of these functions is that a group is formed in which the sworn members support and encourage one another in their individual and collective goals and efforts. The great secret of our ancestors was not necessarily their strategies in war or the use of arcane symbols in magic, but rather their mastery of what we wold call today "group dynamics." they knew how to organize in groups which could meet high goals and conquer new lands with *apparent* effortlessness. In fact their successes: as invaders from the steppes, as builders of city states and empires, and as viking raiders, stems from their ability to organize themselves into effective groups. Such an organization should be formed with a minimum of coercion and implied violence. It is through *prestige* that the greatest changes can be made. No greater power is there than that which comes from sovereign power. What is sovereign power and how can you or your groups obtain it?

Such power comes from three sources: 1) knowledge, 2) position, and 3) charisma. Ideally we can have all three, but strength in any one of these can compensate for lacks in the other two. **Knowledge** is the knowledge not only of the lore and myths and legends of the gods, of the runes, and so on, but also of history and general academic fields, and knowledge of humanity and the ways of the world. **Position** is the fact that one holds an office and is seen as fulfilling a certain function in the eyes of his fellows and the rest of the world. He is recognized as being the leader, or a person of a certain type of importance. Titles help designate such persons. **Charisma** is that certain something that some people have and others do not, or they have it in lesser degrees than others. Literally charisma is a Greek word meaning "gift." A man of charisma is gifted by the gods with this essence.

As we look over these three ways to power, we see that only knowledge is something which we can obtain with some degree of regularity and predictability. Charisma is bestowed by the gods, and positions are largely dependent upon other human beings to bestow. Knowledge is something you can obtain on your own and is something that others cannot take away from you. For these reasons it is considered the most royal and sovereign of all powers.

In forming a kindred you will need at least one other sworn brother. Ideally kindreds are not very large groups, but obviously you do need at least one other man to form the group. There is strength in numbers, however. So try to grow your kindred to be as large as you can make it. Forge your bonds deep and true. These are bonds which should transcend the limits of the prison.

This brings us to one of the most important points in this book: What to do when you emerge from inside. Being in prison has been referred to as being in the "belly of the beast." Odin was/will be in the belly of the Fenris Wolf at the *ragnarök*. He will, however, emerge for the beast's belly when his son, Vidharr, avenges him. When you emerge from a gate and for the first time step on free-soil again, you will be confronted, instantly and profoundly with a choice. To return to the ways that landed you in prison in the first place or to voyage forth in a new life, one that you forged in your work with the ancestral ways. No matter what you swear to yourself now and while in prison this often unexpected *moment of truth* will confront you. It is the jaws of the wolf reaching out to re-consume you. **Prepare for this moment.** Resist and destroy the thought which tries to consume you with old negative patterns as it occurs. Your time in prison can be a "gift" for the transformation that others may never have.

All "rites of transformation" or rebirth rituals have three phases: 1) separation, 2) transformation and 3) re-inclusion. For you going to prison if the first, the work you are doing now is the second and the moment of truth and what you do with it as you emerge from the walls of the prison is/will be the third.

Now it is your work to transform yourself and help your brothers in their endeavors to do the same. Later, your work will be similar but you will have to work in a much broader context of the wider world. To be effective in that fight you will have to bring to bear what transformations you have attained. **Beware of the moment of truth ahead and become its master.**

Chapter Nine

Your Rights

As an inmate in a federal, state or county facility, you have certain rights with regard to the practice of religion. These rights vary from state to state locality to locality. It should be part of your work to determine exactly what your religious rights are in the institution in which you find yourself. Once having determined what those rights are, you should then see to it that your institution lives up to the rights you have. There are rights, and then there are privileges. Rights are generally considered to be those things which are a part of your natural constitution as a human being— they are given by the gods, or the "creator." Privileges are things which are granted by other men, by the state or the prison officials. In order to make your religious studies and experience optimal, you should take advantage not only of your rights, but also of any privileges which you might be granted. Assert yourself, but do not be belligerent or disrespectful. Belligerence will likely get you nowhere, in prison or out.

One thing which has proven rather annoying over the years is the number of prisons which do not allow books or literature of any kind to come in which has *runes* of any sort in them. On the one had the religion of Ásatrú/Odinism in general can be practiced perfectly well without recourse to runes, however, the study of the spiritual traditions surrounding the god Odin himself do require the study of runes. Here, I would like to state for the record that the study of runes is essential to the understanding of the religion of the god Odin himself. It always puzzled us as to why prison officials were worried about the runes being used in the capacity of a "secret code"— because the book itself contains the information needed to decode any message written in runes! Any two people can make up their own "alphabet" or other code to pass secret messages, but this is not what the runes are primarily used for. They are religious symbols— akin to the Hebrew letters of Jews or the Arabic alphabet for Muslims. It might be interesting to inquire as of officials in prisons where runes are *verboten as to* whether or not books with Hebrew letters are forbidden to Jewish prisoners, or books with Arabic letters (e.g. the Koran) are forbidden to Muslim prisoners. If they are not, then runes should, by all rights, be allowed to Ásatrú prisoners.

Unfortunately at this time we here at Rûna-Raven cannot engage in letter-writing campaigns on behalf of prisoners who are having trouble with their institutions. Rûna-Raven is a business and we do what we can to offer good books to prisoners and deal with you as best we can under often difficult circumstances.

In the future we will be opening up a new organization, one called the *Wodharrow Institute*, to prisoners. It is a non-profit organization for those who have an interest in the preservation, promotion and growth of education in the traditional cultural knowledge relating to the Germanic and Indo-European peoples. It is the goal of the Woodharrow Institute to promote traditional fields of academic study relating to Germanic and Indo-European studies. It is our belief that the preservation of these studies where we find them, and their restoration where they have disappeared, will be of great benefit to society at large as we become increasingly aware of the deep cultural values from which we sprang. It is our ever increasing lack of awareness of our "culture of origin" that has led us to boredom within and conflict without. It is the goal of the Woodharrow Institute to provide access to academic and scientific research and methods to its general membership.

If you want to be put on the mailing list to receive information on the Woodharrow Institute, send your address care of the Runa-Raven Press address.

Glossary

This glossary of technical words used throughout the text of this book indicates the exact definitions of words that might be used in unfamiliar ways. Here Old English (OE) or Old Norse (ON) terms from which some of these technical terms are ultimately derived are also given.

Ase, pl. Æsir [pron. "ace"]: The gods and goddesses of consciousness in the Germanic pantheon, governing the powers of sovereignty and physical force. (ON *Áss*; pl. *Æsir*)

Asgard: The enclosure of the gods, and the protected realm where the gods and goddesses exist. (ON *Ásgarðr*)

athem: The "breath of life," the vital force of life borne in the breath. (OE *æthm.*)

blessing: The act of sacrificing and distributing the powers of the gods and goddesses in Midgard. (OE *blôtan* and *bletsian*, to sacrifice.)

boast: A ritual drinking to the honor of a god, goddess, or ancestor, or drinking to seal an oath for actions to be done. Also, a "toast." (OE *bêot.*)

call: The part of a ritual in which the divine forces to take part in the blessing are invoked.

dis, pl. dises: One of the collective ancestral goddesses of the family, clan or tribe. (ON *dís*, pl. *dísir*)

drinking: The part of a ritual in which the liquid loaded with the divine forces is ingested by the gathered folk.

earth: 1) The natural, physical aspects of the universe, 2) The planet Earth, 3) soil.

etin: A giant, ancient inhabitants of the world preceding the advent of the Æsir. (ON *jötunn*)

folk: The Germanic nation (all people of Germanic heritage), 2) The people gathered for a holy event.

frith: Similar to grith, peace, security and well-being

Germania: Used to designate all of the Germanic peoples regardless of geographical location— the Germans, Scandinavians, and English. Also the title of a book about the Germanic peoples written by the Roman historian Tacitus in 98 CE.

giving: The part of a ritual in which the remainder of the loaded liquid not consumed by the gathered folk is returned to the divine realm. Also called the "yielding."

goodman: In a ritual in which active roles are divided, this is the one most responsible for the ritual actions and manipulations of the sacred objects. (OE **godmann*)

grith: Similar to frith, peace, security and well-being.

hallowing: the part of a ritual in which the space in which the ritual is to be performed is marked off from the profane world, made holy, and protected.

harrow: 1) An outdoor altar usually made of stone, 2) A general term for the altar in a true working. (OE *hearg*).
hof: A temple structure, also used as a gathering place for feasts.
holy: There are two aspects to this term: 1) That which is filled with divine power, and 2) That which is marked off and separate from the profane.
hugh: The cognitive part of the soul and the seat of and volition; the intellect or "mind." Also called "hidge." (OE *hyge*.)
hyde: Image, or "shape," of the body. ON *hamr*.
leaving: the formal closing of a ritual.
loading: The part of a ritual in which the sacred power that has been called upon is channeled into the holy drink.
lore: The tradition in all its aspects.
lyke: The physical part of the soul-body (psychophysical) complex. Also called "lich." (OE *lic*.)
Midgard: The dwelling place of humanity, the physical plane of existence. Also, Mid-Yard, the enclosure in the midst of all. (OE *Middangeard*.) Meddlert.
myne: The reflective part of the soul, the memory: personal and transpersonal. (OE *mynd*, ON *minni*.)
nightly: Sometimes used instead of "daily."
reading: The part of a ritual in which a mythic-poetic text is recited in order to place the gathering into a mythic time/space, to engage in the mythic flow of timelessness.
rede: The part of a ritual in which the purpose for the working is clearly stated. The word literally means "counsel" or "advice."
shope: In a ritual in which the active roles are divided, this is the one most responsible for the speaking of the words designed to set the mythic and social context. (OE *scôp*.)
soul: 1) A general term for the psychic parts of the psycho-physical complex, 2) The postmortem shade. (OE *sawl*.)
stall: An indoor altar, especially one that is backed up against an interior wall. (ON *stalli*.)
symbel: The sacred ritual feast at which boasts are drunk. (OE *symbel*.)
theal: In a ritual in which the active roles are divided, this is the one most responsible for the speaking of the words designed to engage the mythic and divine powers. (OE *thyle*.)
tide: A time, occasion, a span of time with a definite beginning and end.
The most prominent example of the survival of this term is in the expression "Yule-tide."
troth: Religion, being loyal to one's own gods and goddesses, and to one's own ancestors, and cultural values of those ancestors. (ON *trú*, OE *treowth*.)
true: Adjective form of "troth" can mean "loyal." A "true man" is a man loyal to the gods and goddesses of his own ancestors.
Van: p. Vanir: The gods and goddesses of organic existence in the Germanic pantheon, governing the realms of organic production, eroticism, wealth, and physical well-being. (ON *Van*; pl. *Vanir*.)
wight: A being or entity of any spiritual kind.

world: The psycho-chronic human aspects of the manifested universe. (OE *weoruld*, "the age of a man." The cosmos.

wyrd: The process of the unseen web-work of synchronicity and case and effect operating on a grand scale throughout the cosmos. Same as weird.

Bibliography

Auld, Richard. "The Psychological and Mythic Unity of the God Odinn." *Numen* 23:2 (1976), pp. 145-160.
Bauschatz, Paul C. "The Germanic Ritual Feast." In: *The Nordic Languages and Modern Linguistics 3*, Ed. John M. Weinstock. Austin: University of Texas Press, 1976, pp. 289-294.
——————. *The Well and the Tree: World and Time in Early Germanic Culture*. Amherst: University of Massachusetts Press, 1982.
Benveniste, Emil. *Indo-European Language and Society*, tr. E. Palmer. Coral Gables, FL: University of Miami Press, 1973.
Branston, Brian. *Gods of the North*. London: Thames & Hudson, 1955.
——————. *The Lost Gods of England*. London: Thames & Hudson, 1957.
Buchholz, Peter. "Schamanistische Züge in der altisländischen Überlieferung." Diss. Münster, 1968.
Caesar, Juilius. *Commentarii de Bello Gallico*. Commented upon by Friedrich Kraner and W. Dittenberger. Berlin: Weidmann, 1961. 3 vols.
Campbell, Joseph. *The Hero with a Thousand Faces*. (= Bollingen Series17). Princeton: Princeton University Press, 1949.
Chadwick, H. M. *The Cult of Othin*. London: Clay, 1899.
Chaney, William A. *The Cult of Kingship in Anglo-Saxon England*. Berkeley: University of California Press, 1970.
Chisholm, James Allen. *True Hearth: A Practical Guide to Traditional Householding*. Smithville: Rûna-Raven, 1994. ($12.95)
——————. *Grove and Gallows:* . Smithville: Rûna-Raven, 2002. ($18.00)
Cleasby, Richard and Gudbrand Vigfusson. *An Icelandic-English Dictionary*. Oxford: University of Oxford Press, 1957.
Davidson, Hilda R. (Ellis). *The Road to Hel*. Cambridge: Cambridge University Press, 1943.
——————. *Gods and Myths of Northern Europe*. Harmondsworth: Penguin, 1964.
Dumézil, Georges. *The Destiny of the Warrior*, tr. A. Hiltebeitel. Chicago: University of Chicago Press, 1970.
——————. *From Myth to Fiction: the Saga of Hadingus*, tr. D. Coltman. Chicago: University of Chicago Press, 1973.
——————. *Gods of the Ancient Northmen*, E. Haugen, ed. Berkeley: University of California Press, 1973.

Eckhardt, Karl August. *Irdische Unsterblichkeit: Germanischer Glaube an die Wiederverkörperung in der Sippe.* Weimar: Bohlaus, 1937.

Einarson, Stefan. *A History of Icelandic Literature.* New York: Johns Hopkins Press, 1957.

Elliott, Ralph. *Runes: An Introduction.* Manchester: Manchester University Press, 1959.

Eliade, Mircea. *Rites and Symbols of Initiation: The Mysteries of Birth and Re-birth,* tr. W. R. Trask. New York: Harper & Row, 1958.

——————. *The Myth of the Eternal Return, or Cosmos and History,* tr. W. R. Trask. (= Bollingen Series 46) Princeton: Princeton University Press, 1971.

——————. *Shamanism: Archaic Techniques of Ecstasy.* tr. W. R. Trask. (= Bollingen Series 76) Princeton: Pirnceton University Press, 1972.

——————. *A History of Religious Ideas.* Chicago: University of Chicago Press, 1978-85, 3 vols.

——————. "Sjelen i Hedentroen." *Maal og Minne* 1926, pp. 169-174.

Flowers, Stephen E. "Revival of Germanic Religion in Contemporary Anglo-American Culture," *Mankind Quarterly* 21:3 (1981), pp. 279-294.

——————. "Toward an Archaic Germanic Psychology," *Journal of Indo-European Studies* 11:1-2 (1983), pp. 117-138.

——————. *Runes and Magic: Magical Formulaic Elements in the Older Tradition.* New York: Lang, 1986.

——————, ed. *The Galdrabók: A Medieval Icelandic Grimoire.* York Beach, ME: Weiser, 1989.

——————. *Rûnarmâl I: The Rûna-Talks, Summer 1991ev.* Smithville: Rûna-Raven, 1996. ($9.00)

——————. *Ibn Fadlan's Travel-Report as it Concerns the Scandinavian Rûs.* Smithville: Rûna-Raven, 1998. ($7.00)

——————. *Johannes Bureus and Adalruna.* Smithville: Rûna-Raven, 1998. ($10.00)

——————. *The Northern Dawn: A History of the Reawakening of the Germanic Spirit.* Smithville: Rûna-Raven, [forthcoming].

Gennep, Arnold van. *The Rites of Passage,* tr. M. B. Vizedom & G. L. Caffee. Chicago: University of Chicago Press, 1960.

Grimm, Jacob. *Teutonic Mythology,* tr. S. Stallybrass. New York: Dover, 1966, 4 vols.

Grönbech, Vilhelm. *The Culture of the Teutons.* London: Oxford University Press, 1931, 2 vols.

Helm, Karl. "Altgermanische Religion." In: *Germanische Wiedererstehung,* Ed. H. Nollau. Heidelberg: Winter, 1926.

——————. *Altgermanische Religionsgeschichte: Die Ostgermanen* Heidelberg: Winter, 1937, vol II, pt. 1.

——————. *Altgermanische Religionsgeschichte: Die Westgermanen.* Heidelberg: Winter, 1953, vol II, pt. 2.

Hermann, Paul. *Nordische Mythologie.* Leipzig: Engelmann, 1903.

Höfler, Otto. *Kultische Geheimbünde der Germanen*. Frankfurt/Main: Diesterweg, 1934.
——————. *Germanisches Sakralkönigtum*. Tübingen: Niemeyer, 1952.
Hollander, Lee M., tr. *The Poetic Edda*. Austin: University of Texas Press, 1962, 2nd ed.
Ingham, Marion. *The Goddess Freyja and Other Female Figures in Germanic Mythology and Folklore*. Ann Arbor, MI: University Microfilms, 1985.
Jones, Gwyn. *A History of the Vikings*. Oxford: Oxford University Press, 1984, 2nd ed.
Jung, Carl. *The Collected Works*. Princeton: Princeton University Press, 1960-1968, 18 vols.
Larson, Gerald J., ed. *Myth in Indo-European Antiquity*. Berkeley: University of California Press, 1974.
List, Guido von. *The Secret of the Runes*. Trans. and introduced by S. E. Flowers. Rochester, VT: Destiny Books, 1988.
List, Guido. *The Invincible*. Trans. and introduced by S. E. Flowers. Smithville: Rûna-Raven, 1996.
Littleton, C. Scott. *The New Comparative Mythology: An Anthropological Assessment of the Theories of Georges Dumézil*. Berkeley: University of California Press, 1973.
McNallen, Stephen A. *Rituals of Ásatrú: I Major Blots*. Breckenridge, TX: The Ásatrú Free Assembly, 1985.
McNallen, Stephen A. *Rituals of Ásatrú: II Seasonal Festivals*. Breckenridge, TX: The Ásatrú Free Assembly, 1985.
McNallen, Stephen A. *Rituals of Ásatrú: III Rites of Passage*. Breckenridge, TX: The Ásatrú Free Assembly, 1985.
Martin, John S. *Ragnarök: An Investigation into Old Norse Concepts of the Fate of the Gods*. Assen: Van Gorcum, 1972.
Mayer, Elard Hugo. *Germanische Mythologie*. Berlin: Mayer & Müller, 1891.
Much, Rudolf. *Die Germania des Tacitus*. Heidelberg: Winter, 1937.
Neckel, Gustav & Hans Kuhn, eds. *Edda, die Lieder der Codex Regius nebst verwandten Denkmälern*. Heidelberg: Winter, 1962.
Neff, Mary. "Germanic Sacrifice: An Analytical Study using Linguistic, Archeological, and Literary Data." Diss.: University of Texas at Austin, 1980.
Neumann, Erich. *The Origins and History of Consciousness*, tr. R. F. C. Hull. New York: Pantheon, 1954.
——————. *The Great Mother*, tr. R. Manheim. (= Bollingen Series 47) Princeton: Princeton University Press, 1963.
Otto, Rudolf. *The Idea of the Holy*, tr. J. Harvey. New York: Oxford University Press, 1953.
Page, R. I. *An Introduction to English Runes*. Woodbridge: Boydell, 1999, 2nd ed.
Polomé, Edgar C. "Some Comments on 'Völuspá' Stanzas 17-18." In: *Old Norse Literature and Mythology: A Symposium*, ed. E. C. Polomé. Austin: University of Texas Press, 1969.

——————. "The Indo-European Component in Germanic Religion." In: *Myth and Law Among the Indo-Europeans: Studies in Indo-European Comparative Mythology*, ed. J. Puhvel. Berkeley: University of California Press, 1970.

——————. "Approaches to Germanic Mythology." In: *Myth in Indo-European Antiquity*, ed. G. Larson. Berkeley: University of California Press, 1974.

Ranke, Kurt. "Ahnenglaube und Ahnenkult." *Reallexikon der germanischen Altertumskunde* 1:1 (1968), pp. 113-114.

Russell, James C. *The Germanization of Early Medieval Christianity*. Oxford: Oxford University Press, 1994.

Saussaye, P. D. *The Religion of the Teutons*. New York: Ginn, 1902.

Saxo Grammaticus. *The History of the Danes: Books I-IX*. Hilda Ellis Davidson, edition and commentary, Peter Fisher, trans. Woodbridge: Brewer, 1996.

Schier, Kurt. *Sagaliteratur*. (= Sammlung Metzler 78) Stuttgart: Metzler, 1970.

Schröder, Franz Rolf. *Altgermanische Kulturprobleme*. Berlin: de Gruyter, 1929.

Schwarz, Ernst. *Germanische Stammeskunde*. Heidelberg: Winter, 1956.

Steblin-Kaminskij, M. I. *The Saga Mind*, tr. K. H. Ober. Odense Universitetsforlag, 1973.

Strömbäck, Dag. *Sejd*. Stockholm: Geber, 1935.

——————. "The Concept of the Soul in Nordic Tradition." *Arv* 31 (1975), pp. 5-22.

Sturluson, Snorri. *Edda*, tr. A. Faulkes. London: Dent, 1987.

——————. *Heimskringla*, L. M. Hollander. Austin: University of Texas Press, 1964.

Thorsson, Edred. *Futhark: A Handbook of Rune Magic*. York Beach, ME: Weiser, 1984.

——————. *Runelore: A Handbook of Esoteric Runology*. York Beach, ME: Weiser, 1987.

——————. *Runecaster's Handbook: At the Well of Wyrd*. York Beach, ME: Weiser, [1988].

——————. *Northern Magic*. St. Paul, MN: Llewellyn, 1992.

——————. *Rune-Song*. Smithville: Rûna-Raven, 1993. ($19.95)

——————. *Green Rûna: The Runemaster's Notebook: Shorter Works of Edred Thorsson. Volume I (1978-1985)*. Smithville: Rûna-Raven, 1996.

——————. *The Nine Doors of Midgard*. Smithville: Rûna-Raven, 1997, 2nd ed. ($15.00)

——————. *Witchdom of the True: A Study of the Vana-Troth and the Practice of Seiðr*. Smithville: Rûna-Raven, 1999. ($15.00)

——————. *Blue Rûna: Edred's Shorter Works III*. Smithville, Rûna-Raven, 2001. ($11.00)

——————. *A Book of Troth*. Smithville: Rûna-Raven, 2nd revised and expanded edition [forthcoming].

Thümmel, Albert. *Der germanische Tempel*. Halle/Saale: Karras, 1909.

Turville-Petre, E. O. G. "A Note on the Landdísir." In: *Early English and Old Norse Studies*, A. Brown, ed. London: Methuen, 1963.

―――――. *Myth and Religion of the North.* New York: Holt, Rinehart & Winston, 1964.
Vries, Jan de. *Altgermanische Religionsgeschichte.* Berlin: de Gruyter, 1956/57, 2 vols.
―――――. *Altnordisches etymologisches Wörterbuch.* Leiden: Brill, 1961.
―――――. *Altnordische Literaturgeschichte.* Berlin: de Gruyter, 1964, 2 vols.

Note: Generally disregard the dollar amounts next to some of the titles in this bibliography. Some of the titles originally published by Rûna-Raven are now available from LODESTAR. Write to LODESTAR for a catalog and further information. Please include two postage stamps to receive a copy of the catalog:

LODESTAR
P.O. Box 16
Bastrop, Texas 78602

www.ingramcontent.com/pod-product-compliance
Lightning Source LLC
Chambersburg PA
CBHW051716040426
42446CB00008B/910